DATE DUE

Harper Lee:
To Kill a Mockingbird

~Writers and Their Works~

Harper Lee:
To Kill a Mockingbird

ANDREW HAGGERTY

 **Marshall Cavendish**
Benchmark
New York

Special thanks to Joan Wylie Hall, professor of English at the University of Mississippi, for her expert review of this manuscript.

Marshall Cavendish Benchmark
99 White Plains Road
Tarrytown, NY 10591
www.marshallcavendish.us

Library of Congress Cataloging-in-Publication Data

Haggerty, Andrew.
Harper Lee : To kill a mockingbird / by Andrew Haggerty.
p. cm. — (Writers and their works)
Includes bibliographical references and index.
Summary: "A biography of writer Harper Lee that describes her era, her major work—To Kill a Mockingbird—her life, and the legacy of her writing"—Provided by publisher.
ISBN 978-0-7614-4280-6
1. Lee, Harper—Juvenile literature. 2. Authors, American—20thcentury—Biography—Juvenile literature. 3. Lee, Harper. To kill a mockingbird—Juvenile literature. I. Title.
PS3562.E353Z69 2009
813'.54—dc22

2008050265

Publisher: Michelle Bisson
Art Director: Anahid Hamparian
Series Designer: Sonia Chagbatzanian

Photo research by Lindsay Aveilhe and Linda Sykes Picture Research, Inc., Hilton Head, SC

The photographs in this book are used by permission and through the courtesy of:
Donald Uhrbrock/Time & Life Pictures/Getty Images: cover, 2, 12, 31;
Lisa Larsen/Time & Life Pictures/Getty Images: 18; AP Images: 25, 41;
Bruce Davidson/Magnum Photos: 34; Chip Somodevilla/Getty Images: 42;
The Everett Collection: 44; Bettmann/Corbis: 49, 54; Universal/The Kobal Collection: 60, 63, 70, 73, 75; Popperfoto/Getty Images: 80; Keystone/Eyedea/Everett Collection: 84;
Ed Clark/Time & Life Pictures/Getty Images: 87.

Printed in Malaysia
1 3 5 6 4 2

Contents

Introduction   6

Part I: Biography and Reputation   9

Chapter 1. Biography   11

Chapter 2. Reputation: Critical
     Reception and Controversy   45

Part II: *To Kill a Mockingbird*   53

Chapter 1. The Novel   55

Chapter 2. Historical Context   81

Works   92

Filmography   93

Chronology   95

Notes   101

Further Information   113

Bibliography   115

Index   120

Introduction

NELLE HARPER LEE is the widely acclaimed author of one of the most important and best-loved works of modern American fiction, her 1960 masterpiece, *To Kill a Mockingbird*. The book was an overnight hit, quickly becoming a best seller; it has been an enduring success as well, and has never gone out of print since its first publication. In 1961 it won the Pulitzer Prize for Literature. For decades it has been regularly taught in high school and college classrooms—a 2008 study found that *To Kill a Mockingbird* is read by more American students in grades 9–12 than any other book. It regularly scores highly on lists of the public's favorite novels: readers voted *To Kill a Mockingbird* fifth on The Modern Library's 1998 "100 Best Novels" list, and in 2006 librarians in the United Kingdom voted it first on a list of "books every adult should read before they die." Lee's publisher, Harper Collins, reports that since its publication, *To Kill a Mockingbird* has "been translated into more than forty languages" and "sold more than thirty million copies worldwide."

In 1962 it was adapted into a movie starring American film icon Gregory Peck, who won an Academy Award for his portrayal of attorney Atticus Finch, the character whose quiet integrity stands at the center of the novel's moral universe. The film is now considered a classic. Although Harper Lee never wrote another book, by any measure few writers have achieved greater success over the course of their entire careers than Lee has attained with her single novel.

The enduring appeal of *To Kill a Mockingbird* no doubt owes much to its accessibility, especially to younger readers. It is not long; the paperback edition, which is what most people read, runs less than three hundred pages. Neither is it a particularly difficult read. While Lee handles the narrative with considerably more deftness than some critics have given her credit for, the tone is warm, often humorous, and always engaging. It is devoid of the technical fireworks for which other American Southern writers, such as William Faulkner, are well-known. But the fact that the novel can be read as easily by readers new to serious fiction as by literary scholars does not mean that the novel is unsophisticated.

Rather, Lee's decision to tell the story largely based on the understanding of a preadolescent child, young Scout Finch, allows her to depict very complex, very dark, very controversial issues of race, violence, and injustice with a powerful, clear-eyed honesty. Scout's character starkly contrasts with the viciousness and racism that pervade her hometown, enabling Lee to show us in an urgent, yet quietly compelling, fashion not just how the world Scout is growing up in actually is, but also how it ought to be. Scout loses many comforting illusions over the course of the story, but does not lose her innocence. This may lie at the heart of the novel's appeal. *To Kill a Mockingbird* ultimately reminds us that it is not at all naïve to believe that innocence, sympathy, and kindness can withstand the onslaught of brutality, bigotry, and ignorance. Indeed, nothing else stands a chance in the face of oppression. The simplicity of this insight does not diminish its profundity.

us that preoccupy Maycomb society but tend to baffle S
r Aunt Alexandra comes to live with them, Scout finds
confronted with all sorts of mysterious prescripts as t
ral, proper order of society, none of which seem to her
lligible: "Somewhere I had received the impression that
s were people who did the best they could with the sense
but Aunt Alexandra was of the opinion, obliquely expre
the longer a family had been squatting on one pat
nd the finer it was." Jem points out, this rule would
he Ewells as among the finest folks in Maycomb, as the
d on welfare near the town dump for three generat
cus's attempts to explain to his children why the Finche
ve" other families, undertaken at the behest of his s
s to a rather ignominious end, as his injunction to act
ung lady and gentleman who are the products of "g
ding" and not "run-of-the-mill people" results in Scout
into tears and Atticus telling the children to "forge
cus's code appears to contrast with the concepts of clas

us that preoccupy Maycomb society but tend to baffle S
r Aunt Alexandra comes to live with them, Scout finds
confronted with all sorts of mysterious prescripts as t
ral, proper order of society, none of which seem to her
lligible: "Somewhere I had received the impression that
s were people who did the best they could with the sense
but Aunt Alexandra was of the opinion, obliquely expre
the longer a family had been squatting on one pat
nd the finer it was." Jem points out, this rule would
he Ewells as among the finest folks in Maycomb, as the
d on welfare near the town dump for three generat
cus's attempts to explain to his children why the Finche
ve" other families, undertaken at the behest of his s
s to a rather ignominious end, as his injunction to act
ung lady and gentleman who are the products of "g
ding" and not "run-of-the-mill people" results in Scout
into tears and Atticus telling the children to "forge
cus's code appears to contrast with the concepts of clas
us that preoccupy Maycomb society but tend to baffle
r Aunt Alexandra comes to live with them, Scout finds
confronted with all sorts of mysterious prescripts as
ral, proper order of society, none of which seem to her
lligible: "Somewhere I had received the impression that
s were people who did the best they could with the sense

Part I: Biography and Reputation

us that preoccupy Maycomb society but tend to baffle S
r Aunt Alexandra comes to live with them, Scout finds
confronted with all sorts of mysterious prescripts as t
ral, proper order of society, none of which seem to her
lligible: "Somewhere I had received the impression that
s were people who did the best they could with the sense
but Aunt Alexandra was of the opinion, obliquely expre
the longer a family had been squatting on one pat
nd the finer it was." Jem points out, this rule would
he Ewells as among the finest folks in Maycomb, as they
d on welfare near the town dump for three generat
cus's attempts to explain to his children why the Finche
ve" other families, undertaken at the behest of his si
s to a rather ignominious end, as his injunction to act
ung lady and gentleman who are the products of "g
ding" and not "run-of-the-mill people" results in Scout b
into tears and Atticus telling the children to "forge
cus's code appears to contrast with the concepts of clas

us that preoccupy Maycomb society but tend to baffle S
r Aunt Alexandra comes to live with them, Scout finds
confronted with all sorts of mysterious prescripts as t
ral, proper order of society, none of which seem to her
lligible: "Somewhere I had received the impression that
s were people who did the best they could with the sense
but Aunt Alexandra was of the opinion, obliquely expre
the longer a family had been squatting on one pat
nd the finer it was." Jem points out, this rule would
he Ewells as among the finest folks in Maycomb, as they
d on welfare near the town dump for three generat
cus's attempts to explain to his children why the Finche
ve" other families, undertaken at the behest of his si
s to a rather ignominious end, as his injunction to act
ung lady and gentleman who are the products of "g
ding" and not "run-of-the-mill people" results in Scout b
into tears and Atticus telling the children to "forge
cus's code appears to contrast with the concepts of clas
us that preoccupy Maycomb society but tend to baffle S
r Aunt Alexandra comes to live with them, Scout finds
confronted with all sorts of mysterious prescripts as t
ral, proper order of society, none of which seem to her
lligible: "Somewhere I had received the impression that
s were people who did the best they could with the sense

Chapter 1

Biography

Monroeville and Family

Nelle Harper Lee was born in Monroeville, Alabama, on April 28, 1926. "Nelle" is the backward spelling of the first name of her maternal grandmother, Ellen Rivers Williams. While family and friends refer to her by her first name (which in an Alabaman accent sounds like "Nail"), she asked her publisher to omit her first name on the front cover of *To Kill a Mockingbird* out of concern that it would be mispronounced as "Nellie," a mistake that had always bothered her. Hence, the public knows her primarily as Harper Lee.

Monroeville is the seat of Monroe County, located in the southern part of the state, not far from the Florida border. For a fairly small city Monroeville has achieved a remarkable amount of literary fame, not least because it is so clearly the real-life Maycomb, Alabama, that provides the setting for *To Kill a Mockingbird*. Lee's childhood friend Truman Capote—widely seen as the model for the character of Dill—also grew up there. Capote became famous for his own semi-autobiographical novel *Other Voices, Other Rooms* (1948), which features a character based on Lee. Capote also wrote the novella *Breakfast at Tiffany's* (1958), which was made into a popular film, and the nonfiction novel *In Cold Blood* (1966), a project for which Lee did much of the research. Later Monroeville natives who became literary figures are the contemporary novelist and journalist Mark Childress and the syndicated newspaper columnist Cynthia Tucker, who in 2007 won the Pulitzer Prize for Commentary.

HARPER LEE SITS ON THE PORCH WITH HER FATHER, THE MAN AFTER WHOM ATTICUS, THE HEROINE'S FATHER IN *TO KILL A MOCKINGBIRD*, IS MODELED.

The citizens of Monroeville by and large seem quite proud of their literary heritage, particularly their association with *To Kill a Mockingbird*. In the 1960s the courthouse in the town square—the site of the fictional trial of Tom Robinson—was scheduled for demolition; townspeople rallied to save it. Since 1991 Monroeville residents have performed an annual stage adaptation of *To Kill a Mockingbird* at the courthouse, an event that draws a local crowd as well as many tourists and fans of the novel.

Lee is the youngest daughter of father Amasa Coleman Lee, familiarly known as "A. C. Lee," and mother Frances Cunningham Finch Lee. In many ways, her father closely resembles Atticus Finch, hero of *To Kill a Mockingbird*— whose last name comes from her mother's maiden name. The son of a Confederate veteran of the Civil War, A. C., like Atticus, was for many years an Alabama state legislator as well as a respected civil attorney. Upon leaving school as a teenager, A. C. first made his living as a schoolteacher and a bookkeeper. After establishing himself as a lawyer he bought a part ownership in the local newspaper, the *Monroe Journal*, and wrote its weekly editorials. There he expounded upon such favorite topics as the need for governmental fiscal responsibility, the problems of the town's economy, and, especially, the dangers of alcohol. His devout, traditional Methodist background made A. C. a lifelong teetotaler, though his most famous daughter would not follow in his footsteps in this regard. One of the interesting differences between A. C. and his literary counterpart is that A. C. did not drink alcohol as a matter of religious and moral principle, while Atticus merely disliked the taste.

A. C. Lee could appear to outsiders as quite aloof and formal, in the manner of most men of his social class and professional standing at the time. Other children especially could find him "intimidating." But at home he put his stiff public bearing aside, becoming an affectionate parent who did not stand on ceremony. Just as Scout calls her father "Atticus," Lee called her father "A. C." And just like her heroine, as a small child Lee liked nothing better than to curl up on her father's lap and read the newspaper. In later life A. C. Lee was not averse to signing autographs with the name "Atticus Finch," showing that he was at least amused and perhaps flattered by his novelistic alter ego, even if his daughter's fictional portrait of him is more a loving transformation than an exact mirror image.

Lee's relationship with her own mother was, sadly, troubled. Frances Lee, like her husband, came from traditional Southern stock. Her father was the postmaster of Finchburg, a settlement on the banks of the Alabama River founded by the Finch family; this is the "Finch's Landing" of *To Kill a Mockingbird*, where Scout has her disastrous Christmas visit with her aunt and cousin. Frances's mother was the daughter of a wealthy plantation owner. Her education stressed decorum above all else, especially when it came to the requirement for a woman to always comport herself as a "lady." Frances Lee learned this lesson well and throughout her life was known as a strict observer of the time-honored codes of acceptable female behavior. Her daughter Nelle Harper, however, like Scout Finch, preferred overalls to dresses as a child and also had a tomboyish allergy to such feminine pursuits as "playing with small stoves [and] tea sets." Scout's antagonistic attitude toward her Aunt Alexandra owes something to her creator's conflict with her mother on the subject of girls and "gentle breeding."

But there were deeper problems. Frances Lee seems to have had bipolar disorder. She could lavish attention and kindness on her children one moment, but become sullen and withdrawn the next. At school she had been something of a musical prodigy. As an adult she would sometimes play the piano for hours on end, completely oblivious to anything else; she could likewise retreat into a book, or sewing. More alarmingly, she could become manic, running to the porch and calling out nonsensically to passersby in the street. Her condition worsened as she aged, and neighbors recall that a time came when her erratic behavior forced her family to keep her almost constantly confined indoors. A good deal of the responsibility for caring for Nelle Harper Lee, the youngest child, fell upon Hattie Belle Clausell, a black woman who was hired to come to the house in the afternoons to clean, cook, and make sure that the young girl was bathed and dressed in clean clothing. Clausell is very likely fondly memorialized as the Finchs' beloved housekeeper, Calpurnia. Lee's mother died in 1951 after suffering from a variety of health problems.

Charles J. Shields, who wrote a biography of Lee with which she did not cooperate, speculates that Scout and Jem's lack of a mother in *To Kill a Mockingbird* parallels the maternal absence that Lee must have felt as a result of her own mother's unfortunate condition. Her mother was not there for her in many ways, and Lee simply had no way to re-create a relationship that had never really existed. But it should be noted that Lee did not seem to blame her mother for any disconnection. She reacted furiously when a 1988 biography of the recently deceased Capote quoted him as declaring that her mother had twice tried to drown her in a bathtub when she was a toddler. In a letter to a friend Lee denied the story as a scurrilous falsehood and attributed it to a persistent "paranoia" that had ultimately overcome her childhood friend in his final years and had gradually driven them apart. In this letter she recalls her mother as a "gentle soul." According to Shields, Lee's oldest sister, Alice Finch Lee, also sharply rebuffed the drowning story when it was repeated by a radio broadcaster.

Alice was born in 1911. Her family nicknamed her "Bear," and, it would appear, deservedly so, owing to her fierce determination and resolve. Alice was perhaps never quite the nonconformist her youngest sibling was as a child, but she was always extremely driven and ambitious, earning top grades and a reputation as a hardworking student. She graduated from high school at sixteen and attended the Women's College of Alabama in Montgomery, but left after her freshman year. A. C. wanted help running the newspaper he had just purchased, and asked her if she would come home to work as associate editor and partner (he gave her a quarter ownership stake). He had entered the state legislature three years previously, and increasingly needed help at home. Frances Lee's condition was deteriorating, and both she and the younger children needed more attention than a housekeeper and a father often far away in the state capitol could provide. Alice dutifully returned, remaining in Monroeville for seven years. In 1937 A. C. decided not to run for reelection, and Alice struck out on her own, working for the newly created Internal Revenue Service in Birmingham.

By 1939 one of A. C.'s law partners died, and he had invited Alice to return home, get a law degree, and join the family firm. She did so, passing the bar in 1943. Through perseverance she overcame the stubborn sexism that made it difficult for a professional woman in the South to achieve the same level of respect as her male colleagues, eventually becoming a pillar of the Monroeville community as her father had been before her. She was particularly involved with the Methodist church, locally and regionally; in the mid–1960s she participated in efforts toward ending the segregation between white and black Methodist congregations in Alabama and Florida.

The second-oldest Lee daughter, Frances Louise—usually referred to by her middle name—was born in 1916; she married and moved to Eufala, Alabama. Lee's only brother, Edwin, was born in 1920. As the nearest sibling to her in age, he was close to Lee as both grew up. He became an officer in the Army Air Force, the predecessor of the modern U.S. Air Force. Tragically, he died in 1951 of a cerebral hemorrhage, only about six weeks after his mother's death.

Childhood Friendship

As children, Lee and Truman Capote were inseparable. Capote's mother, Lillie Mae Faulk, was beautiful, extravagant, self-absorbed, and reckless. She had married foolishly, to a man named Archulus Julius Persons, who was something of a salesman, but even more a drifter and hustler. Truman was born in 1924 in New Orleans, but his parents' turbulent marriage did not last past 1931, after unapologetic infidelities by both parties. As a small child Truman was frequently deposited with his relatives—the Faulks—back in Monroeville, where his mother had grown up, for long stretches of time, usually for the summers. By 1930, he was left there year-round, until 1933, when his mother brought him to New York City with her new husband, well-to-do Cuban textile broker Joseph Capote, who legally adopted him and changed his name—and later turned out to be an embezzler. Capote's mother killed herself with an overdose of the sedative Seconal in 1954, soon after her second husband's shady business dealings were discovered and he lost everything.

Adding to the traumatic sense of abandonment the young Capote felt was the fact that he was set apart from his peers by his unique personality. Precociously intelligent, he was able to read and write by the time he turned five; by ten he felt himself driven to write at least three hours a day, as a sort of "obsession." In addition, he was always quite small, had pronouncedly flamboyant mannerisms, and was not very interested in the rough-and-tumble games played by other boys, though he was adept at performing cartwheels and other gymnastic feats.

TRUMAN CAPOTE BECAME FAMOUS JUST BEFORE LEE WITH THE PUBLICA-
TION OF HIS FIRST NOVEL, *OTHER VOICES, OTHER ROOMS*, BUT WITH
HER FIRST AND ONLY NOVEL, HER FAME ARGUABLY ECLIPSED HIS.

Compounding these distinct social disadvantages, his mother, always keenly eager to live down her humble origins, insisted that her son wear the best, most fashionable clothing she could afford, which made him stick out like a sore thumb in the Depression-era South. Scout and Jem's astonishment when they first meet Dill in Miss Rachel Haverford's collard patch, with his "blue linen shorts that buttoned to his shirt" and his "snow white hair" that "stuck to his head like duckfluff," is likely only a small taste of how oddly Capote came across to his Monroeville peers. He was an inevitable target for bullies.

Fortunately, Capote quickly made friends with Lee, his next-door neighbor. She was about two years younger than he was but nevertheless taller and stronger. Lee enjoyed rough-and-tumble games; she is a lifelong sports fan, passionately devoted to University of Alabama football and the New York Mets. Moreover, like Scout, she was not at all shy about getting into fistfights as a reaction to slights upon the honor of family or friends. She became Capote's protector, unafraid to disperse crowds of young boys ganging up on him, rescuing him from harm as he ferociously, if ineffectually, tried to fight back. They became inseparable and spent hours at Capote's aunt's house reading together or playing. Other times they would go into town to visit the courthouse—one of Lee's, and Scout's, favorite activities.

Neither Lee nor Capote conformed to traditional expectations of what a proper Southern child should be, which is probably one of the reasons they got along so well, though there was more to it than that. For one thing, there were not many kids of their age on their block, and so they were thrown together by circumstances. An exception was Jennings Faulk Carter, Capote's cousin, who was closer in age to Lee than her brother Edwin. He was the third member of their little tribe, going along with them on countless adventures—usually planned, or at least instigated, by Capote—that included staging a peculiar version of a carnival sideshow featuring a manufactured "two-headed chicken." The character of Jem in *To Kill a Mockingbird* appears to owe much to Carter and to Edwin.

Capote and Lee were also perhaps linked by their troubles with their mothers: Capote felt abandoned by his, and Lee undoubtedly felt distanced from hers. Much later Lee would remark, enigmatically, that she and Capote "are bound by a common anguish," which may well refer to these maternal wounds, or else merely to their shared sense of not quite fitting in with other children.

Lee, at least, had her father, who for his part liked the young Capote and, characteristically, felt sympathy for the way he had been abandoned by his parents. He enjoyed playing word games with Capote, and gave him a small pocket dictionary that became one of Capote's most treasured possessions. So perhaps A. C. Lee had both children in mind when he brought home an old Underwood typewriter from his office. They soon put it to good use, endlessly writing stories upon it, with one of them dictating and the other painstakingly pecking out the letters on the keyboard. Other children would sometimes join them, but were not permitted to participate in the storytelling, so deep was the two friends' immersion in their imagined universe. It seems likely that they tended to write about the intricacies and minutiae of their small-town universe, filtered through the lens of the adventure stories they loved to devour. Arthur Conan Doyle's Sherlock Holmes mysteries were favorites, as were Edgar Rice Burroughs's Tarzan tales. They were also avid fans of the Rover Boys and the Tom Swift books, enormously successful works of juvenile fiction by Edward Stratemeyer, who also created the Hardy Boys and Nancy Drew franchises. Lee especially loved the *Seckatary Hawkins* series written by Robert S. Schulkers. As a girl, she wrote away for "membership" to the "Fair and Square Club" about which the books' plots revolve. For Lee, Capote, and Carter, these books were not merely to be read, but to be discussed and acted out, just as the children do in *To Kill a Mockingbird*, where Dill, Capote's alter ego, is described as "a pocket Merlin, whose head teemed with eccentric plans, strange longings, and queer fancies."

Early Education

Lee grew up in a highly literate home, and thus learned to read at a very young age. All three of her older siblings read to her, as did both of her parents. In an extremely rare interview conducted in 2006, Lee recalled that she "arrived in the first grade, literate, with a curious cultural assimilation of American history, romance, the Rover Boys, Rapunzel, and *The Mobile Press*." She claims to have taken no particular pride in her accomplishments, stating that she was no different from any of the other children in her neighborhood who filled the lack of entertainment with books. While they did not have many books, the ones they had were treasured and passed around from child to child like precious objects. But as poor as they were in Depression-era Monroeville, they were still much better off than their classmates from the country, who had no access to books outside the classroom. And they were far more privileged than the children of their African-American servants: "In some of their schools, [black] pupils learned to read three-to-one—three children to one book, which was more than likely a cast-off primer from a white grammar school."

Lee arrived at school not only able to read but also full of self-confidence, willing to speak her mind, and unafraid to address her teacher by her first name. She was unimpressed by authority figures and never took to any form of instruction that struck her as illogical or outside her interests. Scout's recollection of her school days is probably Lee's: "They were an endless Project that slowly evolved into a Unit, in which miles of construction paper and wax crayon were expended by the State of Alabama in its well-meaning but fruitless efforts to teach me Group Dynamics." Capote had the same experience. In later life he described being traumatized by his first-grade teacher, who was so furious at his ability to read that she hit him repeatedly over the hand with a ruler, demanding that he recite the ABCs. There would seem to be an echo of this kind of pedagogical attitude in Scout's abject terror when her novice teacher Miss Caroline solemnly orders her to tell her father to stop reading to her at night.

Despite Lee's modesty, it appears that both she and Capote were quite advanced for their ages and thus easily bored by a highly regimented curriculum not designed to cope with precocious intellects or imaginations. Besides, Lee had the example of her parents before her. The world that Lee learned about when her father read to her from the newspaper must have seemed far more interesting and real than Group Dynamics, and her mother's love of great books and classical music must have struck her as more sophisticated and intelligible than the school curriculum.

High School: Encountering Jane Austen

When Lee made it to Monroe County High School, however, she found that there just might be something to the business of education after all. Her English teacher, Miss Gladys Watson, was a revelation. She was strict about grammar, sternly warning students about the perils of the comma splice. But what truly captivated Lee were Watson's classes on the classics of British literature. Lee had always been an insatiable reader, but now her tastes rapidly matured. She never forgot the woman who had opened this door into the wider literary world for her. In 1959, remembering her former teacher's keen eye for ungrammatical prose, Lee asked Mrs. Watson-Burkett (she had since married) to proofread the manuscript of *To Kill a Mockingbird*. In 1965, after the book and its film adaptation had made Lee wealthy, she invited Mrs. Watson-Burkett to accompany her on a month-long trip to England. There they had ample opportunity to make pilgrimages to the places where the writers Lee had come to love in high school had lived.

Among these authors were Joseph Fielding, who wrote *Tom Jones*, the essayist Charles Lamb, and Samuel Butler. However, she reserved perhaps her greatest affection and esteem for the early–nineteenth-century writer Jane Austen, who is widely considered one of the greatest novelists in the English language. The high school library had a copy of Austen's *Pride and Prejudice*, and it appears that Lee read it over and over again. There can be no doubt that Austen was a major influence for Lee. After *To Kill a Mockingbird* was published Lee was asked about her artistic goals, and she replied, "All I want to be is the Jane Austen of south Alabama."

There is a certain dry irony in the remark, as Lee undercuts the chutzpah of her ambition to be placed on the same level as a literary giant with the wryly humble comment that this is "all" she wants. This sort of understated humor is very much like Austen's. Austen is never harsh or denunciatory; she trusts the reader to tell right from wrong and avoids heavy-handed moral judgments. Even when she is at her most satirical, she extends more pity than anger toward her targets, however foolish or conniving they may be.

The tenor of *To Kill a Mockingbird* is very much like this, particularly when Atticus Finch calmly reminds Scout and Jem that even someone bent on lynching a prisoner in the town jail, or on lying in court to doom an innocent man to execution, is still a human being and must be understood as such. Austen's works do not feature situations as dangerous or dark as these, but they still warn of the dangers inherent in failing to extend sympathetic understanding toward others. Critic Jean Frantz Blackall notes that "the underlying values and themes operative in their [Austen's and Lee's] fictional worlds transcend time and place."

Austen and Lee also share a delight in poking fun at all forms of snobbery. The scene in Lee's book depicting the absurd pretensions of the ladies in Aunt Alexandra's missionary circle is a clear literary descendant of any number of similar scenes in Austen's fiction. Beyond that, Lee admired and sought to emulate Austen's genius for bringing to life all the social rules and customs of a particular era and class. In her post-publication interview for *To Kill A Mockingbird* Lee stated, "There is a very definite social pattern in [Southern] towns that fascinates me. I would simply like to put down all I know about this because I believe that there is something universal in this little world, something decent to be said for it, and something to lament in its passing." Austen is famous for writing exclusively about the lives and manners of the English country gentry, particularly young women's lives. *To Kill a Mockingbird* likewise remains tightly focused on small-town, Southern, middle-class culture. But a restricted setting does not necessarily indicate a restricted view of human nature, if it is observed honestly and intimately enough. Lee took this lesson to heart.

College and University

After graduating from high school in 1944, Lee attended Huntingdon College in Montgomery, where her older sister Alice had gone, although then it was called the Women's College of Alabama. As the name indicates, Huntingdon was an all-women's school. Affiliated with the United Methodist Church, the college stressed propriety as much as academics, and expected its students to behave with the utmost decorum. Lee, though, had never been one for decorum. While Alice had thrived at Huntingdon, her more Bohemian sister ran into difficulties caused by her fondness for smoking and salty language. By the end of her first semester her roommates had kicked her out; by the end of the year she had had enough

TO KILL A MOCKINGBIRD SHARES AT LEAST ONE THING WITH PRIDE
AND PREJUDICE: BOTH ARE STILL WIDELY READ BY TEENAGERS.

and left for the University of Alabama. It is likely that she had agreed to attend Huntingdon in order to please her father, whom she adored, and her sister, whom she respected.

Her father made no secret that he would be more than pleased to have a second child join him in the family businesses, the law firm and the newspaper, as Alice had already done. But Lee was nursing a private dream. She wanted to become a writer, and though she was shy about showing her work to her family, she already had privately produced stacks of material. Truman Capote was not the only young person from Monroeville who felt driven to write. In 1945, Capote's career took off when his first published short story appeared in *Mademoiselle* magazine; the story won an award the following year. It is reasonable to believe that Lee felt that anything her childhood companion could do, she could do just as well, if not better.

Going to the University of Alabama, therefore, may well have seemed a fair compromise between her heart and her family. Upon her arrival she joined a sorority, but after a year she had abandoned it. She found a more congenial atmosphere in the offices of the university's humor magazine, the *Rammer Jammer*, which took its title from a traditional Crimson Tide football cheer. Lee began by writing articles and ended up becoming the publication's editor. Her pieces were largely parodies of the various absurdities of campus life, though she also contributed more serious, if often pointedly sarcastic, material to the university's newspaper, the *Crimson White*.

In one book review she took exception to novelists who felt compelled to discuss Southern slavery and racism either too romantically or too grotesquely, singling out Harriet Beecher Stowe, Lillian Smith, and William Faulkner as guilty of such faults: "The South has been repeatedly embarrassed by the Smiths . . . , Faulkners, Stowes, et. al., who either wrote delicately of the mint julep era or championed the dark eddies of 'n---ertown.'" It is interesting that Lee, no racist herself, should have objected to these authors in particular, as each of them in their own fashion clearly opposed racism and saw slavery as a terrible evil that had wholly corrupted Southern society. However, it is not uncommon for a young, ambitious author to try to stake out artistic turf through a critique of writers with already established reputations.

Lee objected to these writers' works not because they challenged racial stereotypes and abuses, but because in her opinion they did so in an overblown, overdramatic fashion that she thought of as unrealistic. Lee was skeptical of the Southern Gothic genre: novels and plays that depict the South as grotesque and tormented, haunted either figuratively or literally by the ghosts of its sinful past. Southern Gothic writing is often set in eerie, half-ruined plantation houses; plots often feature dark family secrets, incest, rape, or racial violence (or all of these at once). To be sure, the writers most usually associated with the Southern Gothic mode, such as Faulkner and playwright Tennessee Williams, had serious artistic and social purposes. Yet their works are pervaded with an aura characteristic of nineteenth-century supernatural fiction. Certainly, too, Dill is very familiar with *Dracula*, and Scout and Jem are excited to hear his summary of the movie.

It is worth noting that Truman Capote's first book, *Other Voices, Other Rooms*, which would be published two years after Lee's review, is usually seen as a classic Southern Gothic novel. Lee, who had probably seen parts of Capote's manuscript, may have been intent on fashioning a style that would be distinct from his. She may have realized that if she were to become a writer too, her work would inevitably be compared to that of her former playmate and next-door neighbor. Her aesthetic opinions were, of course, sincere; she was genuinely too down-to-earth to be drawn toward the Gothic. It is likely that she was already aware of the need to discover an artistic voice

and sensibility that would clearly distinguish her own stories from those written by someone whom she knew was
bound to draw on much of the same material.

Aspiring writers must, naturally, solve the problem of
making what they have to say sound original. And there
is no doubt that Lee was an aspiring writer at this point,
telling the *Crimson White* in an interview that she would
"probably write a book someday." However, during college Lee was already thinking seriously about taking a
new approach to Southern fiction—an approach *To Kill a
Mockingbird* would later embody. Though her novel does
share some of the typical elements of the Southern Gothic
style, including a rape, an attempted murder, and the eerie
figure of reclusive Boo Radley, the narrative never quite
fulfills the expectations these elements raise. The "rape" is
falsely alleged; Bob Ewell's attempt to murder the Finch
children is foiled. It turns out that Boo Radley is not a
monster at all, but a kind man who has long been misun-
derstood and ill-treated. The novel's humorous and
humane tone also contrasts with the Gothic mode—so
much so that it is possible to see the book as a critique of
a Gothic sensibility. In Lee's American South, violence and
racism are acknowledged as horrible realities, but are not
the entire story.

Leaving College

In 1946, during her junior year, Lee was accepted into the
University of Alabama law school. She was still following
the path her family wished her to pursue, though it seems
she was doing so with increasing reluctance. Because the
workload was so heavy, after a year she was forced to
resign from *Rammer Jammer* and ceased writing regularly
for campus publications. Classmates recall that she did
not seem to be enjoying her courses very much. There
were apparently rumors that she had fallen in love with a
professor, though there is no concrete evidence to support
such speculation. The prospect of letting down her father,

combined with the knowledge that she simply did not want to become a lawyer, appears to be more than sufficient explanation for any unhappiness.

It was not surprising, then, that in the spring of 1948 she leapt at the chance to participate in a student exchange program at England's Oxford University for the upcoming summer. The experience proved transformative, probably confirming her determination to write fiction and to expand her horizons beyond those of tiny Monroeville. Her sister Alice commented that Lee "fell in love with England." After she returned at the end of the summer, she spent one final semester at the University of Alabama before leaving without having graduated. In 1949 she followed her childhood friend Truman Capote to New York City, where she continues to live to this day. Though she regularly returns to Alabama to stay with Alice for a large part of the year, her minister Thomas Butts concedes, "She's really a New Yorker."

Writing *To Kill a Mockingbird*

Lee arrived in New York with little money, taking a small apartment where the rent was cheap because the building had no hot water. Her furniture was rudimentary; she made her writing desk out of an old door. She briefly found work at a bookstore, but soon left for a higher-paying job as an airline-ticket clerk, first for Eastern Airlines, and then for British Overseas Airways Corporation (BOAC). She wrote in her free time, concentrating on short stories. Though not a social butterfly by inclination, she made several close friends in literary and cultural circles, a world to which she had access through her connection to Truman Capote, who was both a rising star and very much a social butterfly. Capote relished celebrity and the glittering Manhattan nightlife. He knew everyone and everyone knew him, and Lee would sometimes go along for the ride.

The most significant of her new acquaintances was a young couple, Michael and Joy Brown. He was a songwriter for Broadway shows and she was a former ballet dancer. They took a liking to Lee and frequently invited her over to their townhouse, which was not far from Lee's apartment but worlds away in terms of comfort and style. They read her manuscripts and became convinced that Lee had a real talent, and that the only thing standing in her way was a lack of time to spend concentrating on her work. On Christmas Day in 1956 they gave her an extraordinary gift—a sum of money equivalent to one year's salary at her airline job. Overwhelmed with gratitude, she accepted their offer, insisting however that this was not a gift at all, but a loan. In an article by Lee published in *McCall's* after *To Kill a Mockingbird*'s triumphant reception, she recalled that she was moved not so much by the money, which was certainly welcome, but even more by her friends' faith in her abilities.

Thus motivated, Lee set to work. Only a few weeks before this momentous Christmas she had mustered up the courage to submit several of her stories to a literary agency to see if they would take her on as a client. This decision proved almost as momentous as the financial gift from the Browns. The agents that she chose on the Browns' recommendation, Annie Williams and Maurice Crain, were to become her close friends and faithful representatives. During their first meeting, Crain told her that while her material showed promise it would be easier to sell a novel than a short story.

By the end of January 1957, Lee had several chapters ready to give him: she had made good use of her sudden and unexpected sabbatical. Lee originally titled the work *Go Set a Watchman*, but Crain proposed instead to call it *Atticus*, after the main character. In a publicity interview Lee later explained that she took the name from the

THE COURTHOUSE IN THE FILM VERSION OF *TO KILL A MOCKINGBIRD* LOOKS JUST LIKE THIS ONE IN MONROEVILLE, ALABAMA, WHERE HARPER LEE SAT FOR A PHOTO IN 1961.

Roman man of letters and great friend of the famous orator Cicero, Titus Pomponius Atticus, whom Lee admired for his reputation as a paragon of learning and culture. It is also possible that she saw a consonance between her father's initials, A. C.—the name by which she knew him—and the names *Atticus* and *Cicero*.

In a matter of months the manuscript had been completed and sent to the publishers J. B. Lippincott. Much to Lee's surprise, it was accepted, with the provision that it be substantially rewritten—a rare event, as first submissions by unknown authors are almost always rejected out of hand. One Lippincott editor, Theresa von Hohoff, who went by the nickname "Tay," was particularly impressed by Lee's ability to present a caring, captivating narrative voice. She did not believe the manuscript was ready to publish immediately by any stretch of the imagination, but was convinced that it had enormous potential. Nevertheless it required a good deal of work, as both the plot and the point-of-view seemed disjointed. With much help from the patient and highly professional Hohoff, Lee ultimately solved the first problem by hinging the narrative upon the dramatic courtroom scenes—Lee's memories of watching her father in the Monroeville courthouse served her well here. The issue of the narrative perspective, however, seemed an intractable obstacle.

In the end Lee produced three separate drafts: the first written in the third person, the second in the first person, and the final version in the form in which it was finally published, where Lee alternates between an adult's retrospective perspective—that of Jean Louise Finch grown to maturity—and the direct perspective of the young Scout. The title changed one final time, Lee having decided that she preferred *To Kill a Mockingbird*. In 1959, about two and a half years after Lee began writing it, Hohoff and Lee at last pronounced the book ready.

Like all authors, Lee welcomed the end of her ordeal, during which she regularly moved back and forth between Monroeville and New York with the changing of the seasons. Doing so undoubtedly created difficulties. When she was in Alabama—where she often worked in a room at the country club—she could not meet with her editor, upon whom she had come to depend. But she needed her family as much as she needed her professional relationships and her friends back in New York. And her family needed her. Her father was not in the best of health, and she needed to go back home to deal with "many family problems" during this period.

Kansas and Capote

At the end of 1959, at a point when Lee had a brief period to herself after completing the manuscript of *To Kill a Mockingbird*, Capote approached Lee with a startling request. He had read about a grisly murder case in rural Kansas. Intruders had broken into a remote farmhouse and killed all four family members inside. The police appeared baffled. Something about the crime exerted a powerful fascination for Capote, and he talked the *New Yorker* into sending him to the Midwest to cover the story. But he wanted help; he needed a "researchist," a term he had invented himself. Would his old friend Nelle like to go with him to assist in making contacts, conducting interviews, and taking notes? She agreed: "The crime intrigued him, and I'm intrigued with crime—and boy, I wanted to go." In December 1959 they boarded a train bound for Kansas.

The book that Capote would eventually write about the murders and the capture and trial of the killers, *In Cold Blood*, came out in 1965. Wildly successful, it earned Capote riches and created a literary and cultural sensation, not simply because of the lurid, hair-raising details of the crime, but because of the innovative way in which he told the story. He decided to take the same techniques a writer of fiction would use to create verisimilitude for made-up events, and use them to recount events that had actually happened. He thus claimed credit for inventing what he billed as an entirely new genre, the nonfiction novel.

Today the book is typically regarded as a landmark of modern American literature, even though—or perhaps because—the ethical questions raised by such an enterprise remain deeply controversial. For instance, many characters in *To Kill a Mockingbird* were based upon real people. Boo Radley was based on a man from Monroeville

TRUMAN CAPOTE WAS LEE'S CHILDHOOD FRIEND AND ADULT COLLEAGUE. THEY WORKED TOGETHER ON THE RESEARCH FOR WHAT BECAME CAPOTE'S GROUNDBREAKING TRUE-LIFE NOVEL, *IN COLD BLOOD*.

who did indeed live near Lee, named Alfred "Son" Boleware. But this was a fictional transformation. Lee does not have a character in the book named Son Boleware; she has a character named Boo Radley. Capote used real people as "characters" in a real-life story about actual murders, and thus, at least theoretically, would have no leeway for invention as in a novel. The moral line that he walks between fiction and reality adds an edge to the book that has a lot to do with why it caused so much of a stir.

In regard to Lee, though, Capote never sufficiently acknowledged her contributions to the project. These contributions were not trivial. Their arrival in Garden City, Kansas, the town nearest to the crime scene, was not auspicious. Capote initially seemed every bit as out of place to the locals as he had all those years ago when he first came to Monroeville as a child. He was flamboyant, small, openly gay, and outspoken, and nobody quite knew what to make of him. The law enforcement officials responsible for handling the case initially saw no reason to give him any more access or information than they had granted to other reporters. This was something of a blow to Capote, who had already sensed that there were deep undercurrents to the events that would require a good deal of patient analysis and research to properly understand, much less write about, in the complex fashion that he desired. It was here that Lee proved her worth.

Alvin Dewey Jr., the Kansas Bureau of Investigation agent in charge of the investigation, later recalled that Lee made a first impression almost precisely the opposite of Capote's. She was from a small town herself, and very much attuned to the rhythms and inclinations of small-town life: she was at home in such an environment, while Capote was not, despite his own background. She struck people as down-to-earth, down-home, friendly, and honest, and was able to gain the confidence of the insiders and informants they needed to approach. Once Lee had broken through the initial resistance, Capote could bring to bear his own formidable conversational abilities. He was highly intelligent, and had a knack for drawing out information, and even quite personal revelations, from his sources once he had gained their trust, or at least their grudging respect. But he needed Lee to get him past their initial indifference, at best, or hostility, at worst.

She was valuable in other ways as well. He did not take notes during his interviews, and relied on her to provide impressions or insights that had escaped him, or to recall key details that he had forgotten or passed over as minor. Lee's biographer writes that she was much more skeptical about some aspects of the case than Capote. When it came to the personality of the head of the murdered family, Herbert Clutter, Lee saw him as a harsh man, tight-fisted with his money, and emotionally remote to the point of oppressiveness with his wife and children. Capote, though, needed to heighten the contrast between the innocent victims and the evil killers, and so in the end depicted Clutter as almost implausibly blemish-free. But, differences of interpretation aside, Capote's version of the story depended heavily on Lee's groundwork. She gave him approximately 150 pages of carefully organized typewritten notes, which he used extensively.

Capote dedicated the book to her, "With Love and Gratitude." But the book was also dedicated to Capote's lover, Jack Dunphy. Her efforts as his "researchist" went unacknowledged. According to some who knew Lee, this lack of acknowledgment for the work she had done bothered her a good deal, though she never said so publicly. She continued to remain friends with Capote, even going so far as to help him scout film locations for an adaptation of his book *The Grass Harp* in 1966. Their relationship was burdened, however, by Capote's accelerating alcoholism and drug abuse, which exacerbated his lifelong tendency to lash out emotionally at those closest to him, a likely consequence of his difficult childhood. He died in 1984.

Fame and Film

To Kill a Mockingbird was practically an overnight success when it came out in 1960. Lee herself did not have high hopes that the book would be a hit, later confessing wryly that she had expected nothing more hopeful than a "quick and merciful death at the hands of reviewers" and perhaps some small "public encouragement." The reviews were, in fact, generally positive and praised the book's humor and warmth, though some reviewers complained of an awkward narrative structure.

Two strokes of fortune ensured that *To Kill a Mockingbird* would garner Lee a great deal of public encouragement. The Literary Guild, a major book club, had recommended her novel to their membership as one of its regular selections, and *Reader's Digest* had done likewise, picking it for its popular Condensed Books series. In the early 1960s, organizations like these exerted a tremendous influence over the literary marketplace. Their decision to promote *To Kill a Mockingbird* was nearly a guarantee that the book would become a commercial success. The book rocketed onto the *New York Times* best-seller list and, by the spring of 1961, Lee was a literary celebrity. Perhaps most gratifying was the response she received from her hometown, where the *Monroe Journal* bragged about Lee's remarkable debut, and the small bookshop proudly announced her triumphant return for a celebratory book signing. Her father was present at this occasion, and Lee was overjoyed that he could witness her triumph. After all, the novel was in large part a tribute to him as a father and as a man.

When, in 1961, the Pulitzer Prize committee named *To Kill a Mockingbird* the best American novel of 1960, the novel's claim to artistic legitimacy was sealed. Perhaps most significantly, though, was that while many readers enjoyed *To Kill a Mockingbird*, many others simply fell in love with it. Many novels are published, only a few of them become best sellers, and even fewer win the Pulitzer

Prize. But even among this elite group, few go on to be still widely read in the fifth decade after their publication, or to continually attract new generations of devotees.

Privately, Lee was fatigued by the inevitable demands upon her time and privacy, though this is not at all apparent from interviews or accounts of her public appearances in this period, during which she showed an ingenuous, self-deprecating wit and a willingness to speak about her life, which had inspired the book. In particular, she was not averse to praising her father, telling *Life* magazine in 1961 that his integrity and selfless public service had made him "one of the most beloved men in this part of the state." But on the whole she escaped whenever she could, either to her agents' rustic cottage in Connecticut, or to Monroeville.

She would, however, soon become subject to even more requests from journalists. Some astute producers had become interested in a possible film adaptation of *To Kill a Mockingbird* almost as soon as it became a best seller. The story seemed rich in dramatic possibilities, particularly the courtroom scenes; moviemakers have always been drawn to the inherent theatricality of jury trials.

Also, in 1961 the growing civil rights movement was very much in the news. This was the year of the first Freedom Riders, a group of black and white activists who rode buses through the South in order to protest segregation. In the South blacks and whites were legally prohibited from sitting together on buses or trains, or from using the same facilities, like bathrooms, at bus or train stations. The Supreme Court had recently declared such segregation illegal for interstate transportation, but racial separation laws were still on the books in Southern states, and hard-core segregationists vowed to make sure they stayed that way. In Lee's home state of Alabama, the Riders were met with violence. Thugs, including Ku Klux Klan members, were essentially given a green light by police to stop the protestors with whatever methods they chose, including firebombing and physical assault. In such a climate the story of Atticus Finch's doomed attempt to win justice for Tom Robinson was timely.

The producers who took on the job were Alan Paluka and his partner Robert Mulligan, who would be the director as well. The screenwriter selected to turn the novel into a working script was the playwright Horton Foote, who also became close with Lee. (Foote died in March 2009.) The next step was to find a star willing to play Atticus. Lee initially wanted Spencer Tracy; other possibilities were Bing Crosby, Rock Hudson, and Robert Wagner. But in the end the job went to Gregory Peck and became the defining role of his career. Peck became close friends with Lee during the production of the film, especially after he traveled to Monroeville to get a sense of the town and, in particular, to meet A. C. Lee. Peck incorporated many of Lee's father's mannerisms into his portrayal, like his habit of toying with his pocket watch.

The chief difference between the film and the novel is that the screenplay spends more time on the character of Atticus and the trial, and less on the adventures of the children. For instance, the scene where Jem and Scout read to the dying morphine addict Mrs. Dubose was filmed, but ended up being cut, because Mulligan—and Peck—felt that in the end it would divert too much of the audience's attention away from the story of the trial. The film received generally positive reviews and was a box office success; today it is regarded as one of the classic American films of the early 1960s. In 1963 it received three Academy Awards; Foote won for Best Adapted Screenplay, Peck for Best Actor, and the third award was for Best Art Direction. Lee had made Peck a gift of her father's watch—her father had died on April 15, 1962— and Peck carried it with him as he received his award. Lee remains proud of the film, saying in a public appearance in 2006 that the film version of the novel "is one of the best translations of a book to film ever made."

Life after *Mockingbird*

The publicity schedule for the film of *To Kill a Mockingbird* was grueling and left Lee exhausted. She seemed to have a knack for addressing large groups, and was in demand for talks at schools and colleges. She was also fairly adroit at interviews with the press. Her biographer reproduces a long extract from a 1963 appearance at the Chicago Press Club, where she deftly deflected a barrage of questions with a disarming wit. She replied, for instance, to the suggestion that many might assume that "the name 'Harper Lee' belongs to a man" by saying that she had indeed been invited to Yale University to give a speech, and was told she could stay in the men's dormitory. "I declined that part of the invitation," she said, pausing to smile, "with reluctance."

But no matter how well she might have performed at such events, she did not like doing them, finding inquiries about her personal life—and the endless stream of questions about whether or not she was working on another book—to be wearying. She has not given an in-depth interview since 1964, and has been known to reply to reporters' written requests to speak with her on the record with a terse and emphatic "Hell No." Some reporters do not get the message, however, and have been known to knock on her door out of the blue, hoping to catch her at a rare unguarded and friendly moment. Such journalists all seem to have been greeted with curt responses ranging from icy politeness to a firmly slammed door. But to those whom she meets on her own terms, she can be remarkably kind and approachable, and not at all shy about doing favors such as signing first editions of her book, which makes them valuable on the collectors' market. It seems unquestionably the case that the deluge of attention that

Harper Lee has always been reclusive, but in August 2007 she attended a ceremony inducting baseball player Hank Aaron into the Alabama Academy of Honor. She was elected to the academy in 2001.

IN NOVEMBER 2007, PRESIDENT GEORGE W. BUSH PRESENTED HARPER LEE WITH THE PRESIDENTIAL MEDAL OF FREEDOM. THE AWARD IS GIVEN TO THOSE WHO HAVE MADE REMARKABLE CONTRIBUTIONS TO THE INTERESTS OF THE UNITED STATES.

poured upon her in the wake of *Mockingbird* left her overwhelmed: she once compared it to "being hit over the head and knocked cold." Some writers court fame, but to Lee, it is clearly far more burden than blessing.

As to why she has not produced another book, one can but guess. (She did begin to research another project in the 1980s, which would have been an account of a series of bizarre murders in eastern Alabama, but this never materialized.) Charles Shields argues that one key reason may be that toward the end of the 1960s she began to lose to illness and death her friends and professional colleagues in New York who had been so crucial to the development of *To Kill a Mockingbird*. Particularly devastating was the death of her agent, Maurice Crain, who lost his struggle with cancer in 1970. Another factor may have been the sheer difficulty of topping the tremendous success of her first book, either commercially or artistically. Asked by a bookseller why she had not written another book, she merely responded, "I said what I had to say." She declined the request of her publishers to contribute a new introduction to the thirty-fifth edition of her novel in a letter to her agent Julie Fallowfield, writing, "*Mockingbird* . . . has never been out of print and I am still alive. . . . It still says what it has to say." The publishers printed the letter in the anniversary edition.

In many ways Lee's life resembles that of Jane Austen, her literary heroine. In her day, Austen certainly appreciated thoughtful responses to her work, but she had no desire for fame, preferring a quiet life in the countryside with her family for company. She never married, living most of her adult life with her mother and sister in a small cottage given to them by a wealthy brother. Lee did become famous for *To Kill a Mockingbird*, both as a book and as a movie, but, like Austen, avoids the limelight.

She divides her time between a New York apartment and her sister Alice's home in Monroeville. She almost never speaks to the press. One extremely unusual exception was a brief interview with the *New York Times* in 2006. This marked a special occasion: an award ceremony at the University of Alabama for the best essay on *To Kill a Mockingbird* written by an Alabama high school student. In this interview she revealed that she had been attending these ceremonies since their inception in 2001, that she is quick-witted and has a sly sense of humor, and that she is genuinely moved by how young readers are inspired by her book. Lee may be reclusive, but she is hardly Boo Radley. Like Austen before her, she merely cannot fathom why anyone would want to become a celebrity, values her privacy, and prefers for her work to speak for itself.

THIS *To Kill a Mockingbird* POSTER SHOWS GREGORY PECK, MARY BADHAM, AND PHILLIP ALFORD IN THE ROLES OF ATTICUS, SCOUT, AND JEM.

Chapter 2

Reputation: Critical Reception and Controversy

THE INITIAL REVIEWS of *To Kill a Mockingbird* were on the whole favorable, although not enthusiastic. Several reviewers were bothered by inconsistencies in the book's narrative perspective. Sometimes the story is told by the adult Jean Louise Finch recalling her childhood, and sometimes we seem to see through the eyes of the young Scout Finch experiencing events as they happen. Writing in the *Atlantic*, Phoebe Adams called the narrative "frankly and completely impossible, being told in the first person by a six-year-old girl with the prose style of a well-educated adult." Lee had wrestled with this problem herself, which is why the novel went through three drafts. The mixed perspective of a sometimes mature, sometimes young narrator (using, however, clearly adult language) represents a compromise between more conventional third- or first-person perspectives. Of course, whether or not Lee's choice represents some sort of aesthetic failure is purely a matter of opinion. Many modern films utilize the device of an adult narrator recollecting her or his past self in a voice-over, so the technique that Lee ultimately employed may simply have been unfamiliar to some of the novel's first critics. At any rate, it seems unlikely that most new readers today would even notice that the perspective does in fact shift, much less see this as a flaw. Lee had perhaps just hit on a strategy that put her ahead of her time.

Still, Adams liked the book, calling it "pleasant, undemanding reading"; she felt the children had a certain "Alcottish" charm, thus comparing Lee's novel to Louisa May Alcott's works, which include *Little Women*, and are usually thought of as a classic example of nineteenth-century fiction for young readers. Other reviewers highlighted the book's undeniable humor and the appeal of the close-knit Finch family. This was seen as particularly refreshing because *To Kill a Mockingbird* does indeed represent, at least stylistically, a departure from the Southern Gothic genre that Lee had been critical of during her college years. The immensely influential *New York Times Book Review* congratulated Lee for refusing to pander to "the current lust for morbid, grotesque tales of Southern depravity. Her central characters, the Finches, are a thoroughly decent and happy family." While she was likely pleased by such observations, Lee might also have been somewhat puzzled, as well. Scholar Alice Hall Petry wryly observes:

> One would never know from these effusive reviews that *Mockingbird* included a false accusation of rape, the shooting (seventeen times) of an innocent black man, the acknowledgement of actual incestuous rape, the attempted murder of children, the stabbing to death of the would-be murderer, a man kept prisoner in his own home, and a lynch mob.

It is not surprising that these initial reviews missed the darker elements of the novel. Lee's novel is in several respects genuinely hard to classify. It is serious adult literature that incorporates certain elements of children's fiction; it treats dark themes typical of the lugubrious Southern Gothic mode, but does so in a dry, witty voice that sounds like Jane Austen speaking with an Alabama twang. Repeated readings reveal that *To Kill a Mockingbird* has many layers of meaning.

To its first readers it was the first book from an unknown author; reviewers were not expecting complexity and therefore focused on surfaces. Even after nearly half a century of popularity, literary critics have written relatively little about *To Kill a Mockingbird*—a rather odd situation for a book so often described as a classic. This paucity of attention may be due to a perception that Lee's novel more properly belongs with young-adult fiction than with "serious" literature. That Lee never produced another book may also be relevant; literary critics like to explore how an author develops themes from work to work, and that is impossible to do with Lee.

Nevertheless, the explosive subject of racial injustice lies at the heart of *To Kill a Mockingbird*. It tended to be downplayed in early reviews, but could not remain in the background for long. If Atticus Finch embodies the moral values that Lee intends her novel to champion, these values are primarily expressed through his defense of Tom Robinson, doomed to be found guilty of a crime he did not commit because he is black and his accuser is white. How one judges Atticus's failed defense of Tom against the pervasive and sickening racism of the society Lee so vividly depicts, is ultimately how one will judge the novel. After all, few, if any, issues are as volatile in America as that of race. Moreover, the central incident in Tom's trial is an alleged rape. The style of the novel may be beguiling, but the subject matter touches upon deeply divisive topics.

Hence, once the artistic stature of *To Kill a Mockingbird* was established, it was bound to attract controversy. This was especially so after the novel became a staple of high school English courses, as it did almost immediately after its publication. In 1966 a school district in Virginia pulled it from school libraries on the grounds that it represented "immoral literature," primarily because it discusses rape. A local paper responded angrily, stating that the book indeed had a serious moral purpose. Lee herself contributed a letter to the newspaper declaring, "Surely it is plain to the simplest intelligence that 'To Kill a Mockingbird' spells out in words of seldom more than two syllables a code of honor and conduct, Christian in its ethic,

47

that is the heritage of all Southerners." But she would hardly be able to intervene or even keep track of all of the similar disputes that were to come. *To Kill a Mockingbird* is one of the most frequently censored books in the United States. The American Librarians Association lists it as one of the Top 100 Banned Novels of the Twentieth Century, along with such works as John Steinbeck's *The Grapes of Wrath*, J. D. Salinger's *The Catcher in the Rye*, and Alice Walker's *The Color Purple*.

Objections to *To Kill a Mockingbird* often focus upon Lee's treatment of sexual subjects said to be inappropriate for young readers. The other major reason it attracts opposition is the frequent appearance in the book of the racial slur, "n---er," which is of course highly offensive to African Americans. Mark Twain's *Huckleberry Finn*, another commonly assigned high school text, is often the subject of fierce debate for the same reason.

The artistic justification for the word's use in the novel is, first, that of realism. It was indeed broadly, and thoughtlessly, used in white Southern society of the 1930s, by adults as well as children. But beyond this, defenders of the novel argue that Lee deliberately includes an explicit repudiation of the word. Atticus rebukes Scout for saying it, telling her "it's common"—reminding her that to use such a term ought to be beneath her as a decent person, even if, as she tells him, "'s what everybody at school says." Everyone at school also believes that Atticus is a "n---er-lover" for defending Tom Robinson vigorously, instead of taking the easy way out and defending him half-heartedly. Since he was following Judge Taylor's orders to take Tom as a client, he would not have been blamed for not seriously contesting the charges against him; rather, that would have been expected for an attorney in his position. Atticus is reminding his daughter that she must aspire to do what is right, and that doing what is right is not synonymous with going along with what everyone else is doing. Lee, then, is not endorsing the word, but condemning it by including it in her book.

However, it would be a mistake to conclude that those who object to the use of this slur in the novel are acting in bad faith, or from a desire to stifle artistic freedom. The slur conjures up, after all, a whole history of systematic violence, hatred, and oppression directed at an entire race of people. There is nothing unreasonable in questioning

HARPER LEE AND GREGORY PECK, WHO PLAYED ATTICUS FINCH IN THE MOVIE VERSION OF *MOCKINGBIRD*, TALKED ON THE SET. PECK SEEMED TO EMBODY ATTICUS FINCH, AND THE FILM MADE THE BOOK'S FAME EVEN MORE WIDESPREAD.

its use in a school assignment or in a play. Journalist Steve Garbarino reported witnessing a performance of Monroeville's annual dramatic adaptation of the novel. At the start of the scene when Atticus, with the help of Scout, faces down the lynch mob bent on killing Tom, a car filled with the actors playing the vigilantes screeched to a halt in front of the courthouse, and they piled out, yelling racial epithets. Two black couples, witnessing this, left in disgust. As Garbarino observed, "It may be that the actors appear to be having too good of a time in their roles as a lynch mob." Such a response is hardly incomprehensible. The history of racial violence in America is, after all, a very real and very painful subject.

Contemporary novelist Nichelle Tramble recalls her own powerful aversion to seeing the word *n---er* in *To Kill a Mockingbird* when she was in high school. Later, however, she came to realize that she had displaced onto the novel her resistance to confronting the difficult reality that "the *n---er* of *To Kill a Mockingbird* is still a weapon." The value of the novel, and others like it, is that it helps us to confront uncomfortable truths, much as we might prefer to avoid them.

Law professors and legal scholars form one group of critical readers of Lee's novel who, with only a few exceptions, wholeheartedly endorse its moral message. Legal scholars have produced far more material on *To Kill a Mockingbird* than have literary scholars. Lawyers are often stereotyped in books, plays, and movies as unscrupulous, greedy, and manipulative. Atticus Finch, with his unshakeable integrity, stands as a refutation of this caricature and a vindication of his profession. As Alice Hall Petry writes, "remarkably, the bulk of the criticism on *Mockingbird*, and some of the best, has come not from literary scholars, but from attorneys." Many of these attorneys provide worthwhile information about the relationship between the law and racism in the American South.

Despite the relatively small amount of scholarly material published on *To Kill a Mockingbird* over the past fifty years, literary scholars and critics have recently begun to show increased interest in Lee's novel. The 2006 publication of Charles Shields's biography of Lee, *Mockingbird: A Portrait of Lee*, as well as the publication of solid scholarship in books like Alice Hall Petry's 2007 critical collection *On Harper Lee: Essays and Reflections*, may give rise to further work on the novel in various disciplines. After all, it is a simple fact that an astonishingly large percentage of Americans encounter the book, and sometimes the film as well, in high school. Inevitably, *To Kill a Mockingbird* has become an occasion for serious public conversation about race, a crucial yet frequently uncomfortable subject that is often avoided. For this reason alone, Lee's novel deserves even more thoughtful critical attention than it has yet received.

cus that preoccupy Maycomb society but tend to baffle
er Aunt Alexandra comes to live with them, Scout finds
f confronted with all sorts of mysterious prescripts as
ural, proper order of society, none of which seem to her
elligible: "Somewhere I had received the impression that
ks were people who did the best they could with the sense
, but Aunt Alexandra was of the opinion, obliquely expre
t the longer a family had been squatting on one pat
nd the finer it was." Jem points out, this rule would
the Ewells as among the finest folks in Maycomb, as the
d on welfare near the town dump for three genera
icus's attempts to explain to his children why the Finch
ve" other families, undertaken at the behest of his s
es to a rather ignominious end, as his injunction to ac
oung lady and gentleman who are the products of "g
eding" and not "run-of-the-mill people" results in Scout
into tears and Atticus telling the children to "forge
icus's code appears to contrast with the concepts of clas

cus that preoccupy Maycomb society but tend to baffle
er Aunt Alexandra comes to live with them, Scout finds
f confronted with all sorts of mysterious prescripts as
ural, proper order of society, none of which seem to her
elligible: "Somewhere I had received the impression that
ks were people who did the best they could with the sense
, but Aunt Alexandra was of the opinion, obliquely expre
t the longer a family had been squatting on one pat
nd the finer it was." Jem points out, this rule would
the Ewells as among the finest folks in Maycomb, as the
d on welfare near the town dump for three genera
icus's attempts to explain to his children why the Finch
ve" other families, undertaken at the behest of his s
es to a rather ignominious end, as his injunction to ac
oung lady and gentleman who are the products of "g
eding" and not "run-of-the-mill people" results in Scout
into tears and Atticus telling the children to "forge
icus's code appears to contrast with the concepts of clas
us that preoccupy Maycomb society but tend to baffle
er Aunt Alexandra comes to live with them, Scout finds
f confronted with all sorts of mysterious prescripts as
ural, proper order of society, none of which seem to her
elligible: "Somewhere I had received the impression that
ks were people who did the best they could with the sens

Part II:
To Kill a Mockingbird

THE RELATIONSHIP BETWEEN ADULTS AND CHILDREN IN *TO KILL A MOCKINGBIRD* IS AN ESSENTIAL THEMATIC ELEMENT.

Chapter 1

The Novel

Introduction

In *To Kill a Mockingbird* Harper Lee tells of the events that transpire in the lives of the Finch family and the town of Maycomb between the early summer of 1932 and Halloween night, 1935. The story is told by the grown-up Jean Louise Finch as she recalls her childhood as the tomboyish Scout, a small girl who wears overalls, disdains dresses, and doesn't mind getting into a good fight if she thinks her honor or her family's is at stake. She is five going on six as the novel's action commences, and is going to school for the first time in the fall.

The narrative voice is that of the adult, but we watch the plot unfold through the eyes of the child. This produces an effect like that of a film voice-over, and creates much of the book's humor. Scout is bright, quick, and confident, but often misbehaves; the adult narrator describes the off-kilter beliefs and frequent perplexities of her hot-headed but good-hearted younger self with a wry affection.

Beyond humor, though, it is through this "doubled" perspective that the reader watches Scout learn about her world over the course of the novel. She finds out about the existence of injustice and evil, and the manner in which a decent person must confront these things in order to remain decent. The adult narration preserves Scout's innocent outrage at learning that systematic cruelty exists, but inflects this with her growing, sobering understanding that often it cannot be defeated, only confronted, but that regardless, one need not—and must not—ever surrender to it.

This lesson is embodied in the character of Scout's father, Atticus Finch. Modeled on Lee's own father, Atticus is hardly perfect. He takes on Tom Robinson's defense because he is told to by the court, not out of altruism; he tells his brother Jack, "I'd hoped to get through life without a case of this kind" (93). As some critical readers have observed, this reluctance is not entirely to Atticus's credit. To be sure, Atticus represents the best of those in his social position in his time, but Lee does not depict him as superior to, or apart from, his society or his time. Despite his best efforts he fails to free Tom Robinson. He had always known he would fail and hoped merely to win on appeal. Tom's death—which is essentially a suicide—comes as a blow, but not one that is entirely unexpected. The forces of what he sees as thoroughly irrational racism are too powerful, too entrenched, for him to overcome or, in some ways, even to comprehend. He sadly remarks to Jack, "Why reasonable people go stark raving mad when anything involving a Negro comes up, is something I don't pretend to understand" (93). Lee makes it plain that in the world depicted in the book a vast gulf stands between the concept of justice based on reason and injustice based on prejudice.

Hence, *To Kill a Mockingbird* is a plea for the genuine application of the core liberal value upon which the United States was, theoretically, founded: the equality of all before the law, regardless of inherited status, innate abilities, or race, as Atticus explicitly argues in his closing statement to Tom Robinson's jury. Atticus's failure indicates that the law is nothing more than an abstraction: he declares to the jury that the law is "a living, working reality" (208), but in condemning Tom to death, they prove him wrong. The unreasonable, unwritten "code" (206) of Southern society prevails, as he knows it will, even as Atticus disparages it. These are the codes that cause Mayella Ewell to turn viciously on Tom because she desires him sexually, that cause Bob Ewell to turn viciously on Atticus because of his perceived loss of face during the trial.

Most horribly of all, these codes cause Tom to essentially kill himself because he comes to believe that his white lawyer cannot keep his promise that the white man's laws could ever protect a black man. Tom may have feared that these unwritten laws may pursue him into the Enfield prison yard, making a mockery of Atticus's faith in the law beyond Maycomb to give his client justice. Tom is shot seventeen times while trying to escape by climbing a fence with his one good arm. That the prison guards used excessive force seems quite clear; that they might have executed him and covered it up is hardly beyond the bounds of possibility.

Written into *To Kill a Mockingbird* is a deeper, more subtle argument that the law cannot guarantee justice. Even Gregory Peck's memorable film performance failed to completely acknowledge this interpretation by emphasizing the courtroom drama as opposed to the sheer ineffectuality of Atticus's legal heroics. For in the novel, Lee bluntly concedes that in Maycomb, as in Southern society at large, Atticus is the unreasonable one. There is, after all, a logic to racism—a sadistic logic, but a logic nonetheless. Racism, for instance, can serve economic purposes; if one can invoke racial criteria to obtain labor at costs far below what would otherwise be available on the open market, from a very narrow perspective those who invoke such criteria are behaving rationally.

From a social standpoint, those who believe themselves superior are acting logically when they act in a superior fashion. Why would a superior act as though he is the equal to someone inferior? In refusing this racist logic, Atticus's actions can seem illogical, and this is indeed what Maycomb sees. Why *should* the dominant white culture accept the concept of equality under the law, as Atticus champions? What would possibly be in it for them? Don't they stand to lose all of the material and psychological benefits their position atop the pinnacle of Southern society confers upon them?

The moral argument in *To Kill a Mockingbird* is thus not the naïve one that Atticus makes—even if he is himself not nearly naïve enough to believe it will work—that an appeal to strictly legal values could end the injustices inherent to a society based upon racist principles. Instead, Lee makes a case for reforming all the "rigid and time-honored code[s]" (206) that in truth govern Maycomb, such as the one that Mayella violates and thereby dooms Tom—that a white woman cannot sexually desire a black man—or the one that the prosecutor, Mr. Gilmer, uses to destroy any good impression Tom may have made on the jury—that a black must never, ever, show pity for a white.

Lee calls for reform that will replace the selfishness that undergirds racist assumptions with a sympathy that challenges them. As Atticus advises Scout, "You never really understand a person until you consider things from his point of view . . . until you climb around in his skin and walk around in it" (34). Atticus is telling his daughter to substitute her own, immature sense of how the world ought to be ordered and arranged for that of another. Scout is a child and thus open to such injunctions. Older people, particularly in the very traditional culture depicted in the book, may have more trouble. It is, after all, commonplace to become heavily invested in protecting a sense of how things *should be* by maintaining that that is how they *are*. This is especially so when it comes to matters like that of race, where even the most transparently false and insulting notions (e.g., "all blacks are lazy") can be considered "natural" and go unquestioned.

In the economic context, of course, the idea that whites were "invested" in racial ideology can be taken literally. Ending racism in the 1930s South would have meant a loss of a cheap labor supply or, for poorer whites, increased competition for jobs. White society would also have become suddenly burdened with the responsibility for significant costs, like having to pay for a school system that would educate black children in a manner equal to that provided for white students.

But it would be equally, if less materially, true in a social context. Bob Ewell quite literally has nothing. However, the one thing he does have is his white skin, something he desperately cherishes precisely because he has nothing else of value. Just as his irresponsibility places him in a cockeyed relationship with the law, his racism places him in an upside-down relationship with the black members of Southern society. Tom Robinson, as poor and as imperfect as he is—he has done jail time for fighting—has more than Bob Ewell in every way that should matter. He has a better home, a better family, more money, and far better morals. What he does not have is Bob Ewell's racial identity, and the tragedy of the novel is that this is what kills him.

Lee claims that it is in fact racism, not race, that impoverishes, affecting the mind, the spirit, and even the body. *To Kill a Mockingbird* dramatizes the need for a thorough reform of deeply rooted Southern values. It should be the depths of one's racism, one's ignorance, one's meanness that excludes one from proper society, not one's skin color. The novel represents Lee's attempt to rewrite the unwritten laws that in the 1930s, as in the 1950s, decreed otherwise and created such profound injustice. The key to beginning the process of upending racial codes, the book claims, lies in learning what it means to express sympathy, to "climb around in [somebody else's] skin and walk around in it."

Intertwined Plotlines

As has often been pointed out, the novel has two principal plotlines. The first involves the three children—Scout, Jem (Jeremy) Finch, and their friend, Charles Baker

IN THE EARLY, "INNOCENT" PERIOD OF THE BOOK AND MOVIE, JEM AND DILL ROLL SCOUT ALONG THE STREET IN A TIRE.

Harris, nicknamed for no clear reason "Dill"—and their mysterious neighbor, Boo Radley. The second focuses on the trial of Tom Robinson. These narratives only really intersect at the end of the book, where their complementary lessons are united.

The book begins with a brief discussion of what "started it all" (7). Initially the focus is on the almost three-year chain of events that culminates when Jem Finch, Scout's older brother, "got his arm badly broken at the elbow" (7). It is not until we finish reading the novel that we learn that this storyline actually ends with Boo Radley's rescue of Scout and Jem from attempted murder.

On Halloween night the reprehensible Bob Ewell, outraged at how Atticus had humiliated him in court by proving to the town that he lied in order to frame Tom

Robinson, seeks revenge by assaulting Atticus's children with a kitchen knife. Bob Ewell is the polar opposite of Atticus morally and socially (and the opposite of Tom Robinson morally and racially). Proudly uneducated and ignorant, he is an abominable father. It becomes clear that he has physically abused his own daughter, Mayella, and expects Tom to carry the guilt for his own crime: He wants to absolve himself by transferring the responsibility for his sins to a black man. He means to compensate for his true moral inferiority by invoking a false racial superiority. If Atticus is the best of the South, Bob Ewell is the worst. Atticus aspires to raise Maycomb up to a higher level; Bob Ewell wishes to drag it down with him into the filth where he lives at the town dump. Boo Radley, on the other hand, whose own awful father has kept him virtually a prisoner in his own home, may be seen as the South that needs to emerge from the darkness, to choose which path to follow. He acts to save the children, killing Bob Ewell in the struggle.

In saving the children, Boo takes his place within the community, and in return, earns the community's respect. Lee here once more illustrates how the deep, unspoken "codes" of Maycomb life transcend legal codes. Boo's oddness excludes him from the community for most of the book; he is a part of Maycomb life not as a person, but as an object of gossip and morbid speculation. But that changes when he rescues Jem and Scout, a change that is most powerfully signified when Sheriff Heck Tate makes clear to Atticus that Boo will not face arrest or trial for stabbing Ewell. Sheriff Tate stresses that the official story, the one that he will write down for the public record, will state that in the act of attempted murder Ewell fell on his own knife, killing himself. However, this is clearly not true. Ewell is killed by a dull kitchen knife, yet Sheriff Tate has retrieved a switchblade from the scene of the stabbing, blandly and unconvincingly informing Atticus that he had taken it away from a drunk earlier that night in town.

Although it is not stated in so many words, we are surely intended to understand that Boo grabbed a kitchen knife when he saw Ewell going after the children—with the switchblade. Atticus, who had at first assumed that Jem killed Ewell, needs to be convinced by Sheriff Tate to agree to this deception. Atticus does so, though it clearly goes against his instinctive sense of integrity, because, as Sheriff Tate argues, Boo's motives were pure, and it would be a "sin" to bring Boo into the "limelight" (279) to which any telling of the facts would expose him. In making this argument, and in bowing to it, Sheriff Tate and Atticus welcome Boo into Maycomb, as it were. Boo is not merely to be tolerated, but accepted, even honored.

Boo Radley and His Children

The Boo Radley plot opens with the sudden arrival of Dill in the yard next door to the Finches. Dill is oddly attired in "abominable blue shorts that were buttoned to his shirts" (40) and has a tendency to tell outrageous lies: "he had been up in a mail plane seventeen times, he had been to Nova Scotia, he had seen an elephant, and his granddaddy was Brigadier General Joe Wheeler and left him his sword" (52). But this propensity is pardoned as the consequence of an active imagination, an imagination that comes in handy for their endless reenactments of adventure books, like those of the Rover Boys, Tom Swift, or Tarzan. He offers to marry Scout, but then forgets about it, causing her naturally enough to "beat him up twice" (46). The neighborhood is an exciting world for them, from the tree house in the Finches' yard to the home of Miss Maudie Atkinson, where they are free to roam about and eat her scuppernongs as long as they do not leap on the arbor.

Dill is essentially an abandoned child, left behind in Maycomb with his Aunt Rachel while his parents are off traveling in parts unknown. When Scout asks him about his father at their first meeting, Dill replies, "I haven't got

In *To Kill a Mockingbird* it becomes clear that reality and illusion are often far apart. The shadow of Boo Radley spooks the kids, but the reality saves their lives.

one" (12). His mother eventually remarries so he will have a stepfather. But all of these absent parental figures are distant and emotionally unavailable, buying him books and presents but denying him time and affection. They are baffled by this strange boy who does not play baseball like other boys, but stays in their home and lives in his "dreamy head" (146). Dill runs away in the third summer of the narrative, traveling from Mississippi to Maycomb by train all alone and hiding out under Scout's bed.

It is perhaps this abandonment that causes Dill to become quickly fixated upon Boo Radley, a subject of Maycomb gossip and legend, the "malevolent phantom" (13) of the Radley home on the Finches' block. His real name is Arthur; he is the son of old Mr. Radley, who, Miss Maudie informs Scout, had a reputation as a dour religious fanatic. Boo's troubles began as a teenager when he got into a scrape with the law after he and two cronies were caught backing "around the square in a borrowed flivver" and locking the town's "ancient beadle, Mr. Conner . . . in the courthouse outhouse" (14). He is sentenced to the state industrial school, which is described as "no prison and no disgrace" (15). His father, however, does see this punishment as a disgrace, and cajoles the judge into letting him take Boo home with him, promising to see to it that he never again misbehaves. Boo is released into his humiliated and vengeful father's custody and never again leaves the house, to the town's knowledge. He is only heard from publicly after he stabs his father in the leg with a pair of scissors in an act of momentary madness. But his father refuses to send him to an asylum, or anywhere else.

Even after his father dies and his brother Nathan returns from Pensacola to take ownership of the home, Boo remains confined and hidden. Legends grow up about him: "Boo was six-and-a-half feet tall, judging by his tracks; he dined on raw squirrels and any cats he could catch, that's why his hands were bloodstained. . . . There was a long jagged scar that ran across his face; what teeth he had were yellow and rotten; his eyes popped, and he drooled most of the time" (17). No child would pass the Radleys' home except at a dead run, and no child would chase a ball into the Radley yard from the adjoining school grounds.

For Dill, the Radley place "drew him as the moon draws water" (11–12). He conceives an intense desire to set eyes on Boo, dares Jem to run past the Radleys' gate and touch the house, and invents elaborate reenactments of what they can piece together of the saga of Boo's life to play out in the backyard. Atticus puts a stop to this once he finds out what is going on, but while this discourages Scout, it only spurs Jem and Dill to more daring escapades. On the last night of Dill's second summer in Maycomb he and Jem hatch a scheme to peer inside the windows of the Radley house in hopes of spotting the ghostly Boo. Jem overrides Scout's objections by contemptuously telling her, "I declare to the Lord you're gettin' more like a girl every day!" (56).

The plan goes awry when they are spotted by Mr. Nathan, who, fearing a Negro (as blacks were called then) intruder and inclined to shoot first and ask questions second, fires at them with a shotgun. In the ensuing uproar the children barely escape getting caught by Atticus for what they had done. That Jem had lost his pants trying to get over the Radleys' fence forces them to come up with highly inventive excuses. Dill almost gets them into even hotter water by explaining that they had been playing strip poker, an excuse that horrifies Jem and Scout, who know that their father considers card-playing among the most depraved of vices. Hurriedly they assure Atticus that they were only using matches. Later that evening, heartsick that he has already disappointed his father, Jem sneaks back toward the Radley home to retrieve his pants, only to discover them mended and folded for him.

The Boo Radley story line is clearly intended to be comic for much of the novel. The escapade with Jem's pants is quite funny, as is Dill's utterly serious but thoroughly uncomprehending attempt to smooth the waters by using strip poker as an excuse. The terror that the children feel is genuine, as is their conviction that Boo Radley is a figure of practically supernatural malevolence. But they are, of course, wrong: Boo Radley is nothing more than what he has been made into by a repressive father and an unfeeling brother. But if his life has been twisted, even deformed, that does not mean that he is incapable of human feeling. He is no monster. For all the darkness of his existence he is able to look out for the children who have a life that he has been denied, one provided by a caring parent who gives them freedom and guidance.

Though they do not realize it, he is watching over them. He mends and folds Jem's pants for him, and in a knothole in a tree on the corner of his property he leaves them small treasures: some gum, a pocket watch on a chain, a knife, and little figures of themselves carved from soap. His brother Nathan seals up the knothole with cement, a small act of meanness that causes Jem to weep, much to Scout's amazement. But Boo does not stop watching over them. At the end of the novel as Scout escorts Boo home after he saved her life and Jem's, Scout finally realizes that she, her brother, and Dill have been "Boo's children" (282) all along.

The significance of Boo Radley's character is that he makes a choice. He undoubtedly has been victimized by his father and brother, and to a large degree by Maycomb itself, turned into a figure of fear by people like Miss Stephanie Crawford, the town gossip. He would have all the reason in the world to be offended by the attention paid to him by the children, as Atticus fears. But he does not, for the very simple reason that he places himself "in their skin" and realizes that they would do him no harm and are innocent of malice. They are just curious children, living the childhood he never had. Instead of resenting them for this, he cherishes them. His response to the victimization he experienced as a child is to protect and defend what he sees as good. It may be that these children are the only thing in his life that he *can* see as good. Thus, he reaches out as best he can to help them when he is needed.

His actions at the end of the book are central to Lee's overall theme, as melodramatic as his unexpected heroism might appear. Far from a cliché or an attempt at tacking on a "happy ending" to an otherwise grim plot, Boo's rescue of Jem and Scout might be taken as Lee's subtle attempt to rewrite Gothic novel narratives of Southern culture. As Claudia Durst Johnson writes, in regard to the Boo Radley material especially, "*To Kill a Mockingbird* partake[s] of the Gothic tradition even as the novel engages the Gothic as a subject for critical commentary." Boo's background has all the elements of a classic Southern Gothic horror story, and so he is inevitably transformed, by Maycomb as well as by the children, into the central figure in a horror story.

Horror stories depend upon a certain principle of inevitability: you may not know what it will be or when you will see it, but a horror story is a horror story precisely because you know that *something* horrible is going to happen. But Boo, ultimately, does not play the role that has been assigned to him. This is unusual in the novel, as most characters do end up fulfilling the roles they have been assigned through their social position. Even Atticus does so, albeit unwillingly. Sheriff Heck Tate convinces Atticus to shoot the rabid dog that wanders onto the Finches' street, despite his deep-seated aversion to guns. This aversion seems to stem not only from Atticus's dislike of weapons as a matter of principle, but also from his unwillingness to be known by others—particularly his children—as "One-Shot Finch" (101) instead of as an ordinary man of integrity and decency. But Maycomb forces him back into the heroic role he had long tried to step out of. For Boo, the judgment of the town, and even perhaps of the children, is irrelevant, which is perhaps how he finally escapes from his psychological imprisonment, if not his father's house. Lee is saying that not every tale needs to end as those who are small-minded expect, or demand, even in the South. Boo Radley changes his story, and that offers the hope that others might perhaps do the same.

The Ewells, Tom Robinson, and Unwritten Laws

To Kill a Mockingbird is full of characters like Boo Radley, those who have been cast aside or wounded in some way, and who must decide how to respond—with sympathy or with resentment, with the desire to do what is right or with the desire to cause others harm. Dill is one such character. For all his oddness, he reacts with outraged dismay to the nightmarish injustice of the verdict that condemns Tom Robinson to die. Old Dolphus Raymond is another. He reveals to Dill and Scout that he only pretends to be a drunk so that the town will excuse his preference for living with blacks. But there are other characters who choose differently, including Bob and Mayella Ewell. And then there is Tom, who chooses to act with pity toward someone else (Mayella), someone who indeed is deserving of pity, and so signs his own death warrant.

Scout is in the second grade when she perceives the first signs that all is not well in her innocent world. Another child at school informs her, insultingly, that her father "defended n---ers" (79); in order to not upset Atticus, she restrains herself from fighting him. She punches her insufferable cousin Francis in the teeth at Christmas after he calls her father a "n---er-lover" (88), though she didn't fully understand the insult. Scout tells her father that "Mrs. Dubose . . . would hound Jem over

[Atticus's] n---er-loving propensities" (112). But it is not until the following summer and the commencement of the trial that she learns the full story.

The Ewells live in squalor in a dilapidated shack at the edge of the town dump. The dump lies between the farm where Tom works and his home, so he passes the Ewells' yard regularly. Mayella begins to ask him to do small chores for her, like chopping kindling or carrying water. One evening she asks him into the home to fix a door. He does so, and finds the door is not broken. She asks him to reach up onto a tall "chiffarobe" (186) (a wardrobe or armoire) to bring down a box for her. As he does so, she grabs his legs; he tries to break free without hurting her, but she continues to reach for him, embracing him and kissing him. Her father suddenly arrives and screams at his daughter, calling her a whore. Tom breaks free and flees for his life. Scout later comes to understand his predicament: "He would not have dared to strike a white woman under any circumstances and expect to live so long, so he took the first opportunity to run—a sure sign of guilt" (197).

After Bob Ewell is done beating his daughter, he goes to the sheriff, Heck Tate, and accuses Tom Robinson of raping her. As a white man, especially one with no other reason to feel any pride in himself whatsoever, he could do nothing else. The codes of Southern behavior governing relations between the races, especially regarding sexuality, demand it. Bob Ewell, so used to humiliation, sees his chance to humiliate another and is determined to take it. The fact that Atticus and Judge Taylor humiliate him simply by doing their jobs drives him to a murderous rage.

It is perhaps somewhat difficult today to fully appreciate the situation in which Tom finds himself as soon as Mayella attempts to kiss him, much less the situation Atticus is in when he decides to give Tom a vigorous defense. After all, there is no question that Tom is innocent. He cannot use his left hand, which was maimed in

IN THIS SCENE, ATTICUS FACES DOWN BOB EWELL, THE MAN WHOSE DAUGHTER FALSELY ACCUSED TOM ROBINSON OF RAPING HER. EWELL IS TRYING TO LEAD A LYNCHING MOB AGAINST THE INNOCENT MAN.

an accident when he was young; the bruises on Mayella's face are clearly made by someone who is left-handed—like her father. Neither of the Ewells is even remotely credible as a witness, being ignorant, vain, contrary, and utterly unwilling or unable to place anything above their profound selfishness. Their testimony is contradictory. Yet Atticus manages to achieve nothing more than to cause the jury to deliberate longer than usual before rendering their verdict. This surprises nobody except Jem, who knows something about the law, since he is Atticus's son, but not much about racism, for perhaps the same reason.

The verdict would not have surprised anyone in the 1930s, when the book is set, or in the early 1960s, when it was published. The horrifying case of the Scottsboro Boys shows this all too well, as do later examples of Southern "justice" relating to alleged crimes committed against white women by black men, like the murder of Emmett Till in Mississippi in 1955. The far less well-known trial of Walter Lett in Monroeville in 1933 was likely Lee's actual source for the Tom Robinson trial. All these cases have key features in common with Tom's ordeal. The honor of a white woman is allegedly violated, and the honor of the white community is thus called into question; white vigilantes attempt to take the law into their own hands by lynching the accused; if this fails, an all-white jury ignores any exculpatory evidence and delivers a guilty verdict and condemns the accused man to death.

As soon as Mayella touches Tom amorously, he knows he is trapped; his very flight for his life will be taken as a sure sign of his guilt. Even the reason he gives for entering the Ewell's shack in the first place is used against him. He agrees to help Miss Ewell, he tells the jury under cross-examination from Mr. Gilmer, the prosecutor, because he "felt right sorry for her" (200). This enrages the whites in the courtroom: How dare he get so above himself, feeling pity toward a white woman simply because he knows she has no money and no one to help her about the house, since her father and siblings refuse to do anything? The unwritten laws of Southern society are far more powerful than the written ones. They might dislike Bob Ewell, but the jury will stand with their race, and not on their laws.

Because Atticus is intimately familiar with the Southern code, perhaps the most heroic figure in *To Kill a Mockingbird*, the one who risks the most in order to do what is right, is not Atticus Finch, but Tom Robinson. By stepping onto the Ewell's property at all, as he does repeatedly, he takes an enormous risk. To be sure, he may be motivated to some degree by fear of the consequences of openly defying a request put to him by a white woman. However, he would also have known that these consequences would be far less severe than those of being believed to have any sort of relations with her. His safest course of action would have been to flee the instant she asked him to do a chore for her. But he did not. There is no reason to doubt that he does as she requests for the reason he states in court: he felt sorry for her. Even questions of whether or not to exercise simple pity, or selfless charity, could be matters of life and death for a black man in 1930s Alabama. That Tom does not weigh the dangers to himself more heavily than he does the pity he feels for Mayella shows that he possesses the ability to "stand in someone else's skin and walk around in it"—the highest virtue the novel endorses. The fact that a mob of white men nearly kills him and a jury of white men sentences him to death for his compassion stands as Lee's most cutting indictment of institutionalized Southern racism.

Tom Robinson's fate also has the effect of challenging, if not invalidating, Atticus's entire conception of the law as he explains it to the jury in his closing arguments. He tells the jury that there is one law for all men, black or white. The jury proves him wrong. The rule of law does not extend to all the inhabitants in the world of *To Kill a Mockingbird*.

ATTICUS AND THE MAN HE DEFENDS, TOM ROBINSON, SIT IN COURT
TRYING WHAT WAS THEN IMPOSSIBLE: TO SWAY A SOUTHERN, ALL-WHITE,
ALL-MALE JURY TO BELIEVE THE FACTS RATHER THAN DELIBERATE BASED
ON THEIR OWN BIAS.

When the rule of law fails, only two options for genuine reform remain. Law might be reestablished by an authority beyond the boundaries of Maycomb County, as occurred in Arkansas in 1957 when President Eisenhower ordered 101st Airborne Division troops to escort nine black students, who were being prevented from attending the recently desegregated Little Rock High School by the Arkansas National Guard. At issue was the need for the federal government to enforce the Supreme Court's 1954 ruling in *Brown* v. *Board of Education of Topeka*, that public schools could no longer be racially segregated under a doctrine of "separate but equal." A government that cannot enforce its own laws is not a legitimate government, which is why Eisenhower intervened.

With such intervention absent, what Lee calls for is a revision of the unwritten codes that truly rule Southern society, a reordering of the social hierarchies that prevent the promise of genuine equality under the law from ever being fulfilled.

Judging Atticus: Morphine, Mobs, and Mockingbirds

Atticus takes Tom Robinson's case not merely because Judge Taylor instructs him to, but because, as he tells Scout, "If I didn't I couldn't hold my head up in town, I couldn't represent this county in the legislature, I couldn't even tell you or Jem not to do something again" (80). He instructs his daughter in his own moral code, clearly distinguishing it from the formal law. Scout asks him, "Are we going to win it," and he replies that they will not, but that "simply because we were licked a hundred years before we started is no reason for us not to try to win" (80). This moral code is a "living, working reality" (208) for Atticus, far more so than the law of the courtroom, with which it comes into direct, irremediable conflict.

Atticus's code appears to contrast with the concepts of

THE ONE PERSON WHO ACTS CONSISTENTLY ADULT IS ATTICUS, WHO, IN THIS SCENE, COMFORTS JEM AFTER A TERRIFYING NIGHT.

class and status that preoccupy Maycomb society but tend to baffle Scout. After Aunt Alexandra comes to live with them, Scout finds herself confronted with all sorts of mysterious prescripts as to the natural, proper order of society, none of which seem to her very intelligible: "[S]omewhere I had received the impression that Fine Folks were people who did the best they could with the sense they had, but Aunt Alexandra was of the opinion, obliquely expressed, that the longer a family had been squatting on one patch of ground the finer it was" (132). Jem points out that this rule would qualify the Ewells as among the finest folks in Maycomb, as they had lived on welfare near the town dump for three generations. Atticus's attempts to explain to his children why the Finches are "above" other families, undertaken at the behest of his sister, comes to a rather ignominious end, as his injunction that Scout and Jem act like a young lady and gentleman who are the products of "gentle breeding" and not "run-of-the-mill people" (135) results in Scout bursting into tears and Atticus telling the children to "forget it" (136).

But surely Lee does wish us to draw a distinction between Atticus and those who would condemn an innocent man to death out of irrational racial allegiances, siding with a white man who is a liar instead of a black man who is honest. There is also a definite, and related, distinction to be drawn between those who would determine "proper" social standing based upon inherited position, and those who would assess an individual's worth based upon that individual's actions.

Lee draws such distinctions by the extent of the character's capacity to extend sympathy toward others. This explains Atticus's insistence that Jem make up for cutting down Mrs. Dubose's camellia bushes by reading to her in the afternoons—a punishment that Jem, accompanied by his sister, endures with little grace. Jem, after all, had been provoked, not least by the old woman's insults directed at Atticus for defending Tom Robinson. Yet the point is made when, after her death, Atticus explains that Jem and Scout had been reading to her as a distraction so that she might die free of her addiction to painkillers. "She was the bravest person I ever knew," Atticus tells him (116). Mrs. Dubose becomes for Jem not a demon, but a human, regardless of how she had treated him. The most intense example of sympathy comes at the moment when Atticus confronts the lynch mob outside the jail, and Scout's presence, along with that of Jem and Dill, changes the mob into individual humans.

It is possible to see in Atticus a certain degree of paternalism, particularly in respect to Lee's depiction of the black community. The moment when Reverend Sykes enjoins Scout, "Miss Jean Louise, stand up. Your father's passin'" (214), as Atticus exits the courthouse after losing the trial is somewhat overdone, as this may not be quite the moment for tribute. Perhaps a likelier emotional reaction from the blacks who have just witnessed this legal travesty would not be deferential respect for a white authority figure, no matter how admirable, but incensed fury. The lack of such a response on the part of the black community is one of the more puzzling aspects of the novel. We do not ever see any black characters who are as fully realized as the white characters—except perhaps for Calpurnia, who for all her virtues and individuality remains in a deferential relationship, at least formally, toward the Finches throughout the book. Even though Calpurnia is considered by Atticus to be "a faithful member of th[e] family" (139), the relationship is still that of master and servant.

In some ways the black characters in the novel are too good to be true, even Tom Robinson, whose fate would still be appalling even if he were not so thoroughly innocent. That the black characters in the book show restraint when provoked is, on the one hand, admirable. On the other, the civil rights movement in the American South, or elsewhere, did not achieve its successes because they acted with restraint. For this reason, the reader might have more sympathy for the woman at Calpurnia's church who is rude to Jem and Scout than the narrative seems to expect us to show. Lee, who very much admired Dr. Martin Luther King Jr., may have gone too far in not acknowledging the pent-up fury of the most victimized social group in her novel. King advocated nonviolence, to be sure, but he did not advocate passivity, and the black community in *To Kill a Mockingbird* does seem unrealistically passive. Perhaps Lee thought that depicting an angry reaction on the part of Maycomb's black community would have diminished the moral impact of showing them to have turned the other cheek, as it were. This would be an understandable goal, but one perhaps achieved at the cost of a failure to acknowledge the legitimate sense of outrage that history tells us Southern blacks quite justifiably felt, even if they chose to address their grievances in a nonviolent fashion.

For better or for worse, *To Kill a Mockingbird* is about its white characters and the unwritten laws of white society, unwritten laws that act solely to maintain white privilege and power, and thus cause their *written* laws to ring utterly hollow. Lee's purpose is to repeal these secret codes; to bring them into the open so they can be examined, and discarded; and to render their adherents, in Miss Maudie's words, people of no "background" (236), a potent term of scorn in Southern society. In the system of values that Lee proposes, the greatest sin is the "sin to kill a mockingbird." As Miss Maudie says, "Mockingbirds don't do one thing but make music for us to enjoy. . . . They don't do one thing but sing their hearts out for us" (94).

The sin is of failing to show sympathy to others who have done you no harm and refusing to extend simple human dignity toward others, particularly those who are oppressed, cast out, or otherwise locked away and abandoned.

TO KILL A MOCKINGBIRD IS SET DURING THE GREAT DEPRESSION,
WHICH BEGAN WITH A STOCK MARKET CRASH IN OCTOBER 1929.

Chapter 2

Historical Context

The Great Depression

To Kill a Mockingbird begins in the summer of 1932 and concludes in the fall of 1935. These are the years of the Great Depression, one of the most traumatic periods in American history. The causes of the catastrophe were complex, but most historians agree that an unstable economic situation was devastated by the stock market crash in New York City in October 1929. Many people lost their life savings or their homes; unemployment soared to 25 percent. The Depression only ended fully with the advent of World War II.

Atticus explains to Scout that Mr. Cunningham has to pay him in produce and firewood because "the Cunninghams are country folk, farmers, and the crash hit them the hardest" (21). According to the Alabama Department of Archives and History (ADAH), the hardships faced by farmers like the Cunninghams preceded the stock market collapse, which thus mainly worsened an already difficult situation:

> For most cotton farmers the origins go back to 1920 when the boll weevil and falling cotton prices ruined many farmers and sent the rate of tenancy soaring after several years of decline. By 1930 Alabama contained 207,000 cotton farms, 70 percent of them worked by white and black tenant farmers.

The Cunninghams are not tenants. They do not farm land owned by someone else; however, Mr. Cunningham can only do this at great sacrifice. His land is heavily mortgaged, or held in an entailment, which imposes significant restrictions as to its use because of the financial claims placed upon it. The more urban areas of the state did not fare much better. The ADAH reports, "The Birmingham industrial district was particularly hard hit, with employment declining in the city of Birmingham itself from 100,000 to only 15,000 full time employees. Some national observers contended that Birmingham was the major American city most affected by the Great Depression."

The Maycomb of *To Kill a Mockingbird*, like the Monroeville of Lee's childhood, is typical in that "there was no hurry, for there was nowhere to go, nothing to buy and no money to buy it with, nothing to see outside the boundaries of Maycomb County" (5). References to the various New Deal programs put in place by President Franklin Delano Roosevelt to cope with the crisis arise frequently in the text, as in Atticus's remark that Mr. Cunningham could get a WPA job. The WPA, or Works Progress Administration, was a program that offered government-paid jobs on various public works projects in an attempt to combat unemployment. In Alabama during the Depression, however, far more people had jobs through "the Civil Works Administration (CWA), which employed 129,000 Alabamians at its peak, and the Civilian Conservation Corps (CCC), which employed nearly 67,000 young Alabama men in forestry and recreational work." In addition, the Tennessee Valley Authority brought electrical power for the first time to much of northern Alabama.

As Patrick Chura has documented, some of Lee's references to Depression-era history are anachronistic: The WPA, for example, did not exist until 1935, but it is mentioned in the novel's fourth chapter, which is set in 1933.

Eleanor Roosevelt did not violate segregation law by sitting with black audience members at the Southern Conference on Human Welfare in Birmingham until 1938, but this event is mentioned by Mrs. Merriweather during the fall of 1935.

Nevertheless, the novel is still very much rooted in the Depression in small-town Alabama. Everyone was poor, even the lawyers and doctors, though some people had a "vague optimism," for "Maycomb County had recently been told that it had nothing to fear but fear itself" (6). This invocation of President Roosevelt's famous reassurance to the American people has an ironic resonance in the novel, where Maycomb succumbs to fear and convicts an innocent man.

Racism and the Law

To Kill a Mockingbird is, of course, fiction, but the trial of Tom Robinson is thoroughly plausible by historical standards. The case of the Scottsboro Boys demonstrates this all too well. Despite much speculation that this was the source for Tom's story in the novel, Harper Lee has said it was not, although she did admit that "it will more than do as an example (albeit a lurid one) of deep-South attitudes on race vs. justice that prevailed at the time." Lee's biographer Charles Shields points out that the drama of the Scottsboro Boys affair took place on the national stage and, in this sense, does not quite fit with the kind of story Lee wanted to tell. After all, *To Kill a Mockingbird* is an intimate story of events that take place in just one small town. But the simple fact that the Scottsboro Boys' case unfolded as it did shows how easily an injustice such as the one that befalls Tom could have occurred.

In March of 1931 a group of nine black youths was "riding the rails"—illegally jumping onto a freight car—from Chattanooga to Memphis, Tennessee. During the Great Depression this was a fairly common mode of transportation for the poor who were looking for work, or for

THE CASE OF THE WRONGFULLY CONVICTED SCOTTSBORO BOYS WAS THOUGHT BY MANY TO BE AN INSPIRATION FOR TOM ROBINSON'S TRIAL IN *TO KILL A MOCKINGBIRD*, THOUGH LEE DENIES IT. IN 1933, PROTESTERS MARCHED ON THE WHITE HOUSE ASKING FOR JUSTICE.

escape. A smaller group of white youths was in the same car and a fight broke out; the white youths lost and were thrown from the train. However, they told the nearest stationmaster that they had been attacked, and he alerted the authorities at the upcoming station to board the train and arrest the black youths. Two white women who were also on the train accused the black men of raping them. That evening the governor of Alabama had to call up the National Guard to hold back a lynch mob bent on storming the jail. The nine boys were tried in the small town of

Scottsboro and rapidly convicted. Eight of them were sentenced to death, the customary penalty for rape, especially the rape of a white woman by a black man. The prosecution requested "mercy" for the final defendant, thirteen-year-old Roy Wright. It only suggested life imprisonment because the boy was so young, although another of the accused Scottsboro Boys, Eugene Williams, also thirteen, was sentenced to death. However, eleven members of the jury insisted on the death penalty, while one held out for life in prison. The jurors believed unanimously in Wright's guilt, but were deadlocked regarding the appropriate sentence, so the case ended in a mistrial.

The trial was a farce. As with Tom Robinson's trial, the jury was composed entirely of white men, all of them relatively poor farmers; townsfolk with professional jobs were routinely excused from jury duty at this time. The young defendants were not so fortunate as to be represented by an Atticus Finch. Instead their legal representation consisted of an alcoholic real estate lawyer from Tennessee who was unfamiliar with Alabama law and an elderly lawyer who was several decades removed from trying a criminal case. The two main witnesses were the two women, who, it soon emerged, had worked as prostitutes, and were terrified that they would themselves be arrested on morals charges if they had not claimed rape. There was no reliable forensic evidence to suggest rape had occurred, and no bruises or other signs of struggle.

However, precisely because the accused had been offered such shoddy, inadequate legal counsel, in 1932 the United States Supreme Court voted 7–2 to overturn their convictions. But the Boys' legal ordeals were not over; the trials were recommenced, though this time they were represented by two prominent New York City lawyers, their fees paid for by donations from citizens outraged by the evident miscarriage of justice. At this point one of the women recanted her testimony, although, ironically, the prosecution managed to convince the jury that she had been paid to do so by the Boys' new attorneys, so this dramatic recantation went for naught.

After serving years on death row, two of the Scottsboro Boys were released because they had been too young to be tried as adults when the case took place. Another was freed because the court eventually agreed that his near-blindness made it unlikely that he had committed the crime, as well as the fact that he was not actually in the train car where the alleged crime had taken place. A fourth was released because it was accepted that being almost paralyzed from syphilis likely would have prevented him from carrying out a physical assault. In the end, five of the defendants served significant jail terms. Four were eventually paroled. In 1947, Haywood Patterson, perhaps the best known of the Scottsboro Boys, escaped to Michigan, where the governor refused to allow him to be returned to prison in the South. In 1950 he published a book about his experiences; the following year, however, he was sent back to prison for manslaughter after a barroom brawl in which another man died. He himself died of cancer in 1952.

The Scottsboro Boys trials took place between 1932 and 1938, and the controversy raged over decades. It became a national news story and an international embarrassment for the United States, showcasing the barbarism of Southern "justice" when it came to matters of race and sexuality. It did, however, result in an important Supreme Court victory, which essentially abolished the Southern institution of all-white juries in trials of this nature.

Lee's audience in 1961 would also have been familiar with the shocking case of Emmett Till. In 1955 Till, a fourteen-year-old teenager from Chicago, was sent by his mother to spend the summer with relatives in the small town of Money, Mississippi. One evening he and some friends went into a local grocery store for candy and soda.

While there, he supposedly wolf whistled at the twenty-one-year-old woman who operated the store. Till spoke with a stutter; it has been claimed that his speech impediment was misinterpreted as the whistle.

In any event, Till's actions cannot justify what happened next. For his transgression against Southern racial codes, the woman's husband and owner of the store, Roy Bryant, and his half brother, J. W. Milam, abducted Till from his uncle's cabin, beat him savagely, crushed his skull, gouged out his eye, shot him in the head, bound him with barbed wire to a piece of farm machinery, and threw

IN 1955, FOURTEEN-YEAR-OLD EMMETT TILL WAS SAVAGELY BEATEN TO DEATH FOR ALLEGEDLY WHISTLING AT A WHITE WOMAN. AN ALL-WHITE JURY ACQUITTED THE MURDERERS, WHO HAD NO QUALMS ABOUT ADMITTING TO THEIR CRIME. THIS WOULD HAVE BEEN FRESH IN THE MINDS OF READERS OF HARPER LEE'S POWERFUL NOVEL ABOUT RACIAL INJUSTICE.

his corpse into the Tallahatchie River. His mother had his body brought back to Chicago for burial, where pictures of his body were taken and widely published, causing a tremendous public outcry. The white community in Mississippi became outraged at what it saw as Northern interference in its affairs, and supported the two white defendants. An all-white jury acquitted the murderers on the grounds that the body could not be proven to actually be that of Till, as it was too disfigured. After their acquittal the two killers admitted their guilt to a magazine in return for a payment of $4,000. The outrage caused by the case in the black community, and throughout much of the nation as a whole, provided a powerful impetus to the American civil rights movement.

Biographical Inspirations for Characters and Events in *To Kill a Mockingbird*

Monroeville in the Great Depression of the 1930s certainly offered plenty of fascinating characters and events, many of which seized hold of Lee's imagination and appear, transformed, in the pages of her novel. In some instances the connections between real life and fictionalized events are somewhat indirect. Lee's biographer cites a newspaper story from 1934 reporting a "mad dog warning" issued by the state after three people were bitten, and suggests that this could have inspired the episode in the book where, at Sheriff Heck Tate's urging, a reluctant Atticus shoots a rabid dog in the street in front of his house.

Old Mrs. Dubose, whose shrill insults provoke Jem into cutting down her camellia bushes, seems to have been based on an elderly woman named Mrs. Jones, who lived close to the Lees and was known to shout at passing children. There is no evidence to suggest, however, that Mrs. Jones was a morphine addict or that the Lee children were required to read to her in order to atone for an attack on her shrubbery.

Capote's young aunt, Marie Rudisill, recalls an escapade in which she, Capote, and Lee heard that the Ku Klux Klan was going to hold a rally in a nearby field. Curious, the three of them decided to spy on the proceedings. Capote, however, climbed out too far on a tree, the branch snapped under him, and he fell yelling to the ground, attracting the Klansmen's attention. In their mad dash to escape Capote lost a large piece of his pants on a barbed-wire fence. If the story is accurate, it may prefigure Jem's similar mishap, as he desperately struggles to flee the Radley premises after Mr. Nathan blasts his shotgun at the children.

Other linkages are more definite. Sam Levy, the Jewish shopkeeper of *To Kill a Mockingbird* who shames the Klan members marching past his house by reminding them that he sold them the sheets they were wearing, is likely to have been derived from Lee's recollection of Mr. Meyer Katz, who owned a Monroeville department store. Katz actually *did* sell sheets to the Klan in the 1920s. And, apparently, there really was a pageant for which schoolchildren had to wear costumes representing various agricultural products, including a ham.

More importantly for the overall plot of the novel, however, is that two doors down from the Lees lived Alfred "Son" Boleware, the model for Arthur "Boo" Radley. As with the Radley house in the book, the Boleware's home directly abutted the elementary school playground, and children had a similar terror of chasing any ball hit or thrown onto the property. The young Lee and her friends were just as obsessed with the home and its most reclusive inhabitant as their fictional counterparts. Capote said in a letter to friends that Lee's account of Scout, Jem, and Dill's attempts to bait Boo Radley into showing himself was "literal and true." He even went so far as to assert that Lee did not invent the depiction of Boo leaving fascinating objects in the knot hole of one of the Radleys' oak trees for the children to find, claiming "everything she wrote about it is absolutely true."

Alfred Boleware Jr. was the youngest child and only son of Alfred and Annie Boleware; hence the nickname "Son." The story told about Boo in *To Kill a Mockingbird* is a close echo of what happened to Son. Like Boo, Son got into trouble with the law after engaging in relatively minor teenage mischief: breaking school windows and robbing a drugstore. And, likewise, his father "rescued" him from being sent to the industrial school by taking his son home, where he became a virtual prisoner, a neighborhood curiosity, and the subject of endless lurid gossip and speculation. There is, however, no report of his having stabbed one of his family members. The similarities between the Radleys and the Bolewares were instantly recognizable to residents of Monroeville; the Bolewares were said to be contemplating legal action, although they finally decided against it.

Similarly, a man named Walter Lett probably partly inspired the character of Tom Robinson, the focus of Lee's second plotline. Tom Robinson is falsely accused of rape by Mayella Ewell and her monstrous father, Robert. Since Tom is black and the novel is set in 1930s Alabama, the fact that he is innocent is irrelevant. Despite Atticus Finch's impassioned defense and the flimsiness of the case against him, it is always a foregone conclusion that the all-white jury will find Tom guilty. While Atticus desperately plans an appeal, Tom is shot to death in a hopeless prison escape attempt.

Tom's story resembles Lett's. In 1933 Lett was arrested just south of Monroeville for raping a white woman named Naomi Lowery. The following year he was convicted and sentenced to death, though, as in the novel, the jury took much longer than expected to make its decision, suggesting that a certain amount of doubt delayed the inevitable guilty verdict demanded by the prevailing racism of the period. Not long afterward, however, a group of prominent Monroeville citizens, convinced that Lett was innocent, wrote to the governor and asked him to review the case. The governor commuted the death sentence to life imprisonment. Unfortunately, the stress of living on death row had driven Lett to madness, and he ended his days in a state mental institution. As with Tom Robinson, and several of the Scottsboro Boys, the grotesque nature of the Southern legal system ultimately broke him down. It is not clear if A. C. Lee was one of the citizens who asked the governor for mercy on Lett's behalf, but it is very possible that he was, given his local stature and his personal code of ethics.

Moreover, in 1919, early in his legal career, A. C. Lee had been required by a judge to defend two black men accused of a capital crime against a white person. Like Atticus, A. C. lost his case. His clients were executed and their bodies disfigured: "pieces of their bloody scalps [were] mailed in a gruesome Christmas package to their victim's son." The experience apparently left A. C. Lee deeply shaken, so much so that he never took on another criminal case. He remained quite conservative on racial issues for most of his life, accepting the common concept of essential differences between blacks and whites, and believing in the necessity of racial segregation. But as he grew older, he realized that the old system was deeply unjust and could not be maintained; he was especially troubled by the gerrymandering that prevented blacks from attaining equal political representation.

Like Atticus, A. C. was not a radical reformer on the question of race, although he did share Atticus's dislike of the Ku Klux Klan. However, no matter how conservative he may have been, nobody truly and deeply committed to any kind of humane values who lived in the South during this period could have ultimately failed to conclude that the traditional cultural and institutional mechanisms of racism were morally wrong, and needed to be demolished. A. C. Lee was indeed such a man, despite his limitations. It is precisely this conflict between humane values and entrenched injustice that his youngest daughter chose to depict in her famous novel.

Works

Novels
1960   *To Kill a Mockingbird.*

Articles
1961   "Love: In Other Words," in *Vogue.*
1961   "Christmas to Me," in *McCall's.*
1965   "When Children Discover America," in *McCall's.*
1985   "Romance and High Adventure," in *Clearings in the Thicket: An Alabama Humanities Reader. Essays and Stories from the 1983 Alabama History and Heritage Festival*, edited by Jerry Elijah Brown.
2006   "A Letter from Harper Lee," in *O: The Oprah Magazine.*

Filmography

To Kill a Mockingbird. Dir. Robert Mulligan. Brentwood Productions. 1962.

The film version of *To Kill a Mockingbird* is widely recognized as an American classic. In 1963 it won three Academy Awards: Gregory Peck, for Best Actor; Horton Foote, Best Writing for a Screenplay Based upon Material from Another Medium; and Best Art Direction-Set Decoration, Black and White. It also was awarded three Golden Globes and a prize from the Cannes Film Festival. As he went to the podium to receive his Oscar, Peck carried with him a pocket watch that had formerly belonged to Lee's father, A. C. Lee, the model for Atticus Finch. Lee and Peck remained friends for the remainder of his life; he died in 2003.

Other honors the film has received include several from the American Film Institute (AFI), which recognized Atticus Finch in 2003 as the all time "Number 1 Hero" of American cinema. The AFI has also named *To Kill a Mockingbird* the top courtroom drama of all time (2008) and the twenty-fifth best film of all time (2007). See the AFI's website at www.afi.com for details.

In 2005, at the personal behest of Peck's widow, Veronique, Lee made an exception to her policy of avoiding public appearances when she was honored at a benefit dinner for the Los Angeles Public Library. Her award was presented by actor Brock Peters, who had memorably played the role of Tom Robinson in the film.

Lee also was close to Foote, an accomplished screen-writer playwright, whose screenplay she has consistently praised as faithful to her original vision. She appeared publicly at his ninetieth birthday celebration in New York in 2006. He died in March 2009.

Lee has herself been featured as a movie character in two major motion pictures. In 2005 she was played by Catherine Keener in *Capote*, directed by Bennett Miller, which dramatizes Truman Capote's travels to Kansas for the book *In Cold Blood*, where he is accompanied by Lee as his "researchist." In this film she is presented as possessing a clear-eyed morality and humility while her childhood friend increasingly loses himself in the cheap allure of celebrity and a haze of drug abuse and alcoholism. Lee was, unusually, moved to publicly complain about inaccuracies in the film in letters to the *The New Yorker*, pointing out that the famous *New Yorker* editor Wallace Shawn—who had commissioned the original article on which Capote's book is based—did not accompany Capote to Kansas to witness the execution of the killers, as the movie depicts.

The second film with Lee as a character is *Infamous* (2006), which again re-creates the trip to Kansas with Capote for *In Cold Blood* and the events that occurred in its aftermath. Sandra Bullock plays Lee in this picture. In *Infamous*, Lee is clearly meant to perform much the same narrative function as in *Capote*—Capote's moral foil—but Bullock's Nelle Harper Lee exhibits a sly sense of fun that renders *Infamous* somewhat less obvious and didactic, and more entertaining.

Chronology

1913 Amasa Coleman (A. C.) Lee moves to Monroe-
      ville, Alabama.

1926 Nelle Harper Lee born to A. C. and Frances Lee.

1927 A. C. Lee elected state legislator.

1928 Truman Capote stays with relatives next door to
      the Lee home.

1929 A. C. Lee purchases part ownership of the *Monroe-
      ville Journal* and becomes chief editorial writer.
      Stock market crashes in New York, precipi-
      tating the Great Depression.

1931 Scottsboro Boys arrested, charged with rape of
      two white women.

1933 Walter Lett arrested in Monroeville, charged with
      rape of white woman.

1939 A. C. Lee decides not to run for reelection to the
      state legislature.

1944 Lee graduates from high school, attends
      Huntingdon College in Montgomery.

1945   Lee leaves Huntingdon College, enters University of Alabama, begins writing for university publications.

1946   Lee edits university humor magazine, *Rammer Jammer*.

1947   Lee enrolls in School of Law at the University of Alabama.

1948   Lee attends summer exchange program at Oxford University, England, and leaves law school at the end of the fall semester without taking a degree.

         Truman Capote publishes debut novel, *Other Voices, Other Rooms*, featuring a character based on Lee.

1949   Lee moves to New York City, where she takes work as an airline clerk, writing at night on home-made desk.

1950   Final Scottsboro Boy released on parole.

1951   Lee's mother and brother Edwin die.

1955   Emmett Till lynched in Money, Mississippi, for allegedly flirting with a white woman.

         Montgomery, Alabama, bus boycott breaks out after arrest of Rosa Parks for refusing to surrender her seat to a white man.

1957   Michael and Joy Brown give Lee a year's salary for Christmas so she can devote herself to writing.

1958   Lee presents her agent, Maurice Crain, with the first chapters of what would become *To Kill a Mockingbird*; a complete manuscript is accepted by editor Tay Hohoff of Lippincott Publishers, and extensive period of revising commences.

1959   Final draft of *To Kill a Mockingbird* delivered.
        Lee accompanies Capote as "researchist" for book about the Clutter family murders in Kansas.

1960   Lee completes proofs of *To Kill a Mockingbird*.
        Lee returns to Kansas with Capote for further research as well as to attend the trial of the killers.
        Lee's novel is published, becomes a popular success.

1961   *To Kill a Mockingbird* wins Pulitzer Prize, is sold to film producers.
        "Freedom Riders" protest meets with violence in Alabama.

1962   A. C. Lee dies.
        To Kill a Mockingbird is released as a feature film, directed by Robert Mulligan and starring Gregory Peck as Atticus Finch, with a screenplay by Horton Foote.

1963   Film version of *To Kill a Mockingbird* wins three Academy Awards, including Best Actor for Peck, and Best Adapted Screenplay for Foote.

1964   Lee largely ceases to make public appearances or to give interviews.

               Killers of the Clutter family executed.

1965   Capote publishes *In Cold Blood*, with a dedication to Lee (as well as to Capote's lover, Jack Dunphy).

1966   Upon the recommendation of Gregory Peck, Lee is named to President Lyndon Johnson's National Council of the Arts, serving a six-year term.

1969   Stage adaptation of *To Kill a Mockingbird* by Christopher Sergal published.

1984   Death of Truman Capote.

1990   Lee awarded honorary doctorate by University of Alabama.

2001   Lee inducted into Alabama Academy of Honor.

               Honors College of the University of Alabama begins essay contest on *To Kill a Mockingbird* open to Alabama high school students; Lee attends awards luncheon annually.

2005   Lee portrayed as a character in feature film, *Capote*.

2006   Lee portrayed as a character in feature film, *Infamous*.

2007   Lee awarded Presidential Medal of Freedom, the highest award granted by the United States government to an American citizen, by President George W. Bush.

2009   Horton Foote dies.

us that preoccupy Maycomb society but tend to baffle
r Aunt Alexandra comes to live with them, Scout finds
 confronted with all sorts of mysterious prescripts as
ral, proper order of society, none of which seem to her
lligible: "Somewhere I had received the impression that
s were people who did the best they could with the sense
, but Aunt Alexandra was of the opinion, obliquely expr
t the longer a family had been squatting on one pat
nd the finer it was." Jem points out, this rule would
he Ewells as among the finest folks in Maycomb, as the
d on welfare near the town dump for three genera
icus's attempts to explain to his children why the Finch
ve" other families, undertaken at the behest of his s
s to a rather ignominious end, as his injunction to act
oung lady and gentleman who are the products of "g
eding" and not "run-of-the-mill people" results in Scout
into tears and Atticus telling the children to "forge
icus's code appears to contrast with the concepts of clas

us that preoccupy Maycomb society but tend to baffle
r Aunt Alexandra comes to live with them, Scout finds
 confronted with all sorts of mysterious prescripts as
ral, proper order of society, none of which seem to her
lligible: "Somewhere I had received the impression that
s were people who did the best they could with the sense
, but Aunt Alexandra was of the opinion, obliquely expr
t the longer a family had been squatting on one pat
nd the finer it was." Jem points out, this rule would
he Ewells as among the finest folks in Maycomb, as the
d on welfare near the town dump for three genera
icus's attempts to explain to his children why the Finch
ve" other families, undertaken at the behest of his s
s to a rather ignominious end, as his injunction to act
oung lady and gentleman who are the products of "g
eding" and not "run-of-the-mill people" results in Scout
into tears and Atticus telling the children to "forge
icus's code appears to contrast with the concepts of clas
us that preoccupy Maycomb society but tend to baffle
r Aunt Alexandra comes to live with them, Scout finds
 confronted with all sorts of mysterious prescripts as
ral, proper order of society, none of which seem to her
lligible: "Somewhere I had received the impression that
s were people who did the best they could with the sense

Notes

Introduction

p. 6, par. 1, Mary Pope Osborne, S. E. Hinton, Daniel Handler, and Christopher Paul Curtis, *What Kids Are Reading: The Book-Reading Habits of American Students* (Wisconsin Rapids, WI: Renaissance Learning, 2008), http://www.renlearn.com/whatkidsarereading/Reading Habits.pdf (accessed January 29, 2009).

p. 6, par. 1, Modern Library, "100 Best Novels," The Modern Library, Random House Publishing Group, http://www.randomhouse.com/modernlibrary/100best-novels.html (accessed April 8, 2009).

p. 6, par. 1, Michelle Pauli, "Harper Lee Tops Librarians Must-Read List," *Guardian* (March 2, 2006), http://www.guardian.co.uk/books/2006/mar/02/news.michellepauli (accessed January 29, 2009).

p. 6, par. 1, "About the Book: *To Kill a Mockingbird*," HarperCollins (2009), http://www.harpercollins.com/books/9780060935467/To_Kill_a_Mockingbird/index.aspx (accessed January 29, 2009).

Part I: Biography and Reception
Chapter 1

p. 13, par. 1, Roy Hoffman, "Long Lives the Mockingbird," *New York Times*, August 9, 1998, http://query.nytimes.com/gst/fullpage.html?res=9A04E7DF1038F93AA3575BC0A96E958260 (accessed January 28, 2009).

p. 13, par. 3, Marie Rudisill and James C. Simmons, *Truman Capote: The Story of His Bizarre and Exotic Boyhood by an Aunt Who Helped Raise Him* (New York: William Morrow and Company, 1983), 190.

p. 14, par. 1, Alice Hall Petry, *On Harper Lee* (Knoxville: University of Tennessee Press, 2007), xvi.

p. 14, par. 2, Harper Lee, *To Kill a Mockingbird* (New York: Warner Books, 1987), 86.

p. 14, par. 2, Lee, *To Kill a Mockingbird*, 136.

p. 15, par. 2, Charles J. Shields, *Mockingbird: A Portrait of Harper Lee* (New York: Henry Holt, 2006), 41–42; *See also* Kathy Kemp, "Mockingbird Won't Sing," *News and Observer*, November 12, 2007, http://www.jlc.net/~rwright/pages/leearticle.html. For a discussion of Frances Lee's illness, *see* Shields, 39–42.

p. 15, par. 2, *See* Gerald Clarke, *Capote: A Biography* (New York: Simon and Schuster, 1988), 21–22.

p. 15, par. 2, Shields, 270–271.

p. 16, par. 2, Shields, 126.

p. 17, par. 3, Lawrence Grobel, *Conversations with Capote* (New York: New American Library, 1985), 52.

p. 19, par. 1, Deborah Davis, *Party of the Century: The Fabulous Story of Truman Capote and His Black and White Ball* (Hoboken, NJ: John Wiley and Sons, 2007), 12.

p. 19, par. 1, Lee, *To Kill a Mockingbird*, 12.

p. 19, par. 2, Shields, 284.

p. 20, par. 1, Marianne M. Moates, *A Bridge of Childhood: Truman Capote's Southern Years* (New York: Henry Holt, 1989), 87.

p. 20, par. 1, Petry, xvii.

p. 20, par. 2, Patricia Burstein, "Tiny Yes, But a Terror?" *People*, May 10, 1976, http://www.people.com/people/archive/article/0,,20066445,00.html (accessed February 4, 2009).

p. 20, par. 3, Moates, 37.

p. 20, par. 3, Rudisill and Simmons, 192. Rudisill says that A. C. Lee deliberately gave the typewriter to both Lee and Capote. It is worth noting that Rudisill's book must be treated cautiously, since Capote claimed that "everything" in it "is a lie" (Grobel, 49–50). However, as is often the case with Capote, this assertion may not be altogether true.

p. 20, par. 3, Shields, 46–47. The "Seckatary Hawkins Fair and Square Club" that Lee joined as a child still exists today. You can apply for membership by visiting its home page at www.seckatary.com.

p. 21, par. 1, Lee, *To Kill a Mockingbird*, 12.

p. 21, par. 2, Harper Lee, "A Letter from Harper Lee," *O: The Oprah Magazine*, July 2006, 152.

p. 21, par. 3, Shields, 127.

p. 21, par. 3–p. 22, par.1, Lee, *To Kill a Mockingbird*, 37.

p. 22, par. 1, Grobel, 51.

p. 22, par. 3, Shields, 63–64.

p. 22, par. 3, Shields, 132.

p. 23, par. 1, Shields, 260–261.

p. 23, par. 2, Shields, 105.

p. 23, par. 2, Shields, 64.

p. 23, par. 2, Roy Newquist, ed., "Harper Lee," interview by Roy Newquist, *Counterpoint* (Chicago: Rand McNally, 1964), 412.

p. 23, par. 4, Jean Frantz Blackall, "Valorizing the Commonplace: Harper Lee's Response to Jane Austen," in Petry, *On Harper Lee*, 33.

p. 24, par. 1, Newquist, 412.

p. 24, par. 2, When Lee attended Huntingdon, however, the school did accept male day students, the first of whom graduated in 1934. Huntingdon began accepting residential male students in 1954. For more information, *see* the college's website at http://www.huntingdon.edu/ about_hc/ history.

p. 24, par. 2, Shields, 77.

p. 26, par. 4–p. 27, par. 1, Shields, 90. *See also* W. U. McDonald Jr., "Harper Lee's College Writings,"*American Notes & Queries* 6.9 (May 1968): 131–133.

p. 27, par. 3, Shields, 96.

p. 28, par. 2, Shields, 93.

p. 28, par. 3–p. 29, par. 1, Shields, 104–105. Since one of the sources of the rumor is Capote, it ought to be viewed with skepticism. Capote was not shy about speculating about Lee's possible romantic involvements, though usually without much foundation. On December 3, 1961, Capote wrote to mutual friends that he had "good reason to believe that she [Lee] is unhappily in love with a man impossible to marry etc. And this, combined with several other things, has reduced her to a highly nervous condition" (Clarke, Letters, 332–333). However, not long afterward he wrote back to say that Nelle had only been upset because of her father's recent heart attack (336). Capote also once rather bizarrely said to an interviewer, "That's been the story of [Lee's] life—that I spent my childhood asking her to marry me. I spent my childhood asking her to keep her hands out of my pants. . . . There's more truth than fiction in that" (Grobel, 66). Perhaps even more odd is Capote's cousin Jennings Faulk Carter's remark:

> The only true friend he had that wasn't family was Nelle Harper Lee. When they were children Nelle would comfort him and say, "it's all right, Truman, that you know everything, even if the teachers don't understand." Later Nelle failed him, too. She was the sweetheart image in his young life, but for whatever reasons, at a time when he wanted a sweetheart and a lover, she could not be this. (Moates, 227)

Given Capote's unabashed homosexuality, it is not clear what to make of Carter's assertion. At any rate, there is a complete lack of solid biographical information about any aspect of Lee's romantic life.

p. 29, par. 2, Marja Mills, "To Find a Mockingbird," *Chicago Tribune*, December 28, 2002, http://www.smh.com.au/articles/2002/12/27/1040511175523.html (accessed February 4, 2009).

p. 29, par. 2, Mills, "To Find a Mockingbird."

p. 29, par. 3, Shields, 20.

p. 30, par. 1, Harper Lee, "Christmas to Me," *McCall's*, December 1961, 63.

p. 30, par. 3–p. 31, par. 1, Shields, 114.

p. 32, par. 3, Newquist, 405.

p. 33, par. 1, Clarke, *Capote*, 319.

p. 35, par. 3, Shields, 139.

p. 36, par. 2, Shields, 151–153.

p. 36, par. 3, Shields, 253.

p. 36, par. 3, Claudia Durst Johnson, *"To Kill a Mockingbird": Threatening Boundaries* (New York: Twayne, 1994), xiv.

p. 37, par. 1, Newquist, 405.

p. 38, par. 2, "Literary Laurels for a Novice," *Life*, May 26, 1961, 78A–78B.

p. 40, par. 1, Ginia Bellafante, "Harper Lee, Gregarious for a Day," *New York Times*, January 30, 2006, http://www.nytimes.com/2006/01/30/books/30lee.html?r =1 (accessed February 4, 2009).

p. 40, par. 2, Shields, 223–224.

p. 40, par. 3, Mark Childress, "Looking for Harper Lee," *Southern Living* 32.5, May 1997, 149; *see also* Bellafante.

p. 40, par. 3, Kemp, "Mockingbird Won't Sing"; *see also* Steve Garbarino, "Greetings from Monroeville," *Black Book*, July 30, 2007, http://www.blackbookmag.com/article/greetings-from-monroeville2/996 (accessed February 4, 2009).

p. 40, par. 3, Richard Chalfin, "The Day Harper Lee Came to See Me," *New York Observer*, December 3, 2000, http://www.observer.com/node/43707 (accessed February 4, 2009).

p. 42, par. 1, Newquist, 405.

p. 42, par. 2, Shields, 259–263.

p. 43, par. 1, Chalfin, "The Day Harper Lee Came to See Me."

p. 43, par. 1, Harper Lee, "Foreword," *To Kill a Mockingbird* (New York: HarperCollins, 1993).

p. 43, par. 3, Bellafante, "Harper Lee, Gregarious for a Day."

Chapter 2
p. 45, par. 1, Phoebe Adams, "*To Kill A Mockingbird*, by Harper Lee," *Atlantic Monthly*, August 1960, http://www.theatlantic.com/unbound/classrev/mocking.htm (accessed February 4, 2009).

p. 45, par. 2, Adams, "*To Kill A Mockingbird*, by Harper Lee."

p. 46, par. 1, Frank H. Lyell, "One-Taxi Town: *To Kill a Mockingbird*," *New York Times Book Review*, July 10, 1960.

p. 46, par. 2, Alice Hall Petry, *On Harper Lee* (Knoxville: University of Tennessee Press, 2007), xix.

p. 47, par. 3–p. 48, par. 1, Charles J. Shields, *Mockingbird: A Portrait of Harper Lee* (New York: Henry Holt, 2006), 254.

p. 48, par. 1, American Library Association, "Banned and/or Challenged Books from the Radcliffe Publishing Course Top 100 Novels of the 20th Century," American Library Association Public Information Office, 2008, http://www.ala.org/ala/aboutala/offices/oif/bannedbooksweek/bbwlinks/reasonsbanned.cfm (accessed February 4, 2009).

p. 48, par. 3, Harper Lee, *To Kill a Mockingbird* (New York: Warner Books, 1987), 79.

p. 48, par. 3, Lee, *To Kill a Mockingbird*, 90.

p. 49, par. 2–p. 50, par. 1, For a lucid exposition of the argument for why Lee's frequent use of the word renders her novel unfit for middle school and high school classrooms, *see* Isaac Saney, "The Case Against *To Kill a Mockingbird*," *Race & Class* 45 (July 2003): 99–100.

p. 50, par. 1, Steve Garbarino, "Greetings from Monroeville," *Black Book*, July 30, 2007, http://www.blackbookmag.com/article/greetings-from-monroeville2/996 (accessed February 4, 2009).

p. 50, par. 2, Nichelle D. Tramble, "Full Circle: A Personal Reflection," in Petry, *On Harper Lee*, 35–40.

p. 50, par. 3, For a detailed essay on the critical response to *To Kill a Mockingbird*, see the introduction in Petry, *On Harper Lee*.

p. 50, par. 3, Petry, xxii.

Part II: *To Kill a Mockingbird*
Chapter 1
All text citations reference the 1987 edition of the novel. Harper Lee, *To Kill a Mockingbird* (New York: Warner Books, 1987).

p. 56, par. 1, Perhaps the best-known sustained critique of Atticus Finch as a moral exemplar is by law professor Monroe H. Freedman. "Atticus Finch—Right and Wrong," *Alabama Law Review* 45 (2003–2004): 473. Reprinted in Candice Mancini, *Racism in Harper Lee's "To Kill a Mockingbird"* (Farmington Hills, MI: Greenhaven Press, 2008).

p. 67, par. 2, Claudia Durst Johnson, *"To Kill a Mockingbird": Threatening Boundaries* (New York: Twayne, 1994), 39.

Chapter 2
p. 81, par. 3, Alabama Department of Archives and History, "The Great Depression, The New Deal, and Alabama's Political Leadership," Alabama Moments in American History, http://www.alabamamoments.alabama. gov/sec48det.html (accessed February 4, 2009).

p. 82, par. 1, ADAH, "The Great Depression, The New Deal, and Alabama's Political Leadership."

p. 82, par. 2, ADAH, "The Great Depression, The New Deal, and Alabama's Political Leadership."

p. 83, par. 1, Patrick Chura, "Prolepsis and Anachronism: Emmet Till and the Historicity of *To Kill a Mockingbird*," *Southern Literary Journal* 32.2 (Spring 2000): 3.

p. 83, par. 3, Charles J. Shields, *Mockingbird: A Portrait of Harper Lee* (New York: Henry Holt, 2006), 118.

p. 86, par. 2, For information on the Scottsboro Boys, *see* Douglas O. Linder, "'The Scottsboro Boys' Trials," *Famous American Trials*, 1999, http://www.law.umkc.edu/faculty/projects/ftrials/scottsboro/scottsb.htm (accessed January 30, 2009).

p. 88, par. 2, Shields, 127.

p. 88, par. 3, Shields, 34–35.

p. 89, par. 1, Marie Rudisill and James C. Simmons, *Truman Capote: The Story of His Bizarre and Exotic Boyhood by an Aunt Who Helped Raise Him* (New York: William Morrow and Company, 1983), 171–173.

p. 89, par. 2, Shields, 48. *See also* George Thomas Jones, *Happenings in Old Monroeville*, vol. 1 (Monroeville, AL: Bolton Newspapers, 1999), 135.

p. 89, par. 2, Shields, 33. Marianne Moates writes that "the climactic scenes in Mockingbird" (63) are based on the events surrounding a Halloween party devised by Capote before he left for New York to join his mother. The Klan had heard rumors, inadvertently started by

Capote, that a number of black youngsters would be attending the party, disguised in Halloween costumes. Outraged at the possible race mixing at a party with boys and girls present, they gathered in force and seized one boy headed for the event dressed as a robot. A. C. Lee intervened, however, and after revealing that the child was in fact white, berated the Klansmen for their dangerous foolishness. Humiliated, the masked figures slunk away into the night, never to trouble Monroeville again. The boy was none other than Son Boleware, Lee's model for Boo Radley. According to Moates, "the struggle of Scout Finch in a bulky costume constructed of chicken wire and brown cloth that made it nearly impossible for her to see or walk was probably grounded in poor Sonny Boular's trouble that night with his robot costume" (63). This claim is suggestive, but in the absence of direct confirmation from Lee herself, it should be taken purely as speculation. It is perhaps unusual that an anecdote so dramatic was not frequently repeated by the loquacious Capote. After all, he corroborated the veracity of other sources for *To Kill a Mockingbird*, but does not appear to have mentioned this specific story, even though he is represented as witnessing the episode and, indeed, instigating it. *See* Marianne Moates, *A Bridge of Childhood: Truman Capote's Southern Years* (New York: Henry Holt, 1989).

p. 89, par. 3, Gerald Clarke, *Too Brief a Treat: The Letters of Truman Capote* (New York: Random House, 2004), 290.

p. 89, par. 3, William L. Nance, *The Worlds of Truman Capote* (New York: Stein and Day, 1970), 223.

p. 90, par. 1, Shields, 53–54.

p. 90, par. 1, Shields, 189; Moates, 2.
p. 91, par. 1, Shields, 118–121.

p. 91, par. 2, Shields, 121.

p. 91, par. 3, Shields, 125.

p. 91, par. 3, Shields, 125–126.

Further Information

Books

Agee, James, and Walker Evans. *Let Us Now Praise Famous Men*. Boston: Houghton Mifflin, 2000.

Bloom, Harold, ed. *Harper Lee's "To Kill a Mockingbird."* New York: Chelsea House, 1997.

Johnson, Claudia. *Understanding "To Kill a Mockingbird": A Student Casebook to Issues, Sources, and Historic Documents*. Westport, CT: Greenwood Press, 1994.

Shields, Charles. *I Am Scout: The Biography of Harper Lee*. New York: Henry Holt and Co., 2008.

Websites

http://www.ala.org/ala/aboutala/offices/oif/bannedbook sweek/bbwlinks/reasonsbanned.cfm
"Banned and/or Challenged Books from the Radcliffe Publishing Course Top 100 Novels of the 20th Century." American Library Association. 2008. The American Library Association site provides a fascinating list of the places where *To Kill a Mockingbird* attracted the attention of censors and would-be censors, citing the reasons why the book was denounced.

http://www.english.uiuc.edu/maps/depression/depression.htm
Nelson, Cary. "The Great Depression." *Modern American Poetry.*
An overview of the causes, effects, and international context of the Great Depression, containing statistics, maps, and historical analysis, but with an emphasis upon the catastrophe's impact on American society and culture. Contains a photographic essay rich in imagery of American life in the 1930s.

http://www.law.umkc.edu/faculty/projects/ftrials/scottsboro/scottsb.htm
Linder, Douglas O. "'The Scottsboro Boys' Trials." *Famous American Trials.* 1999.
A comprehensive collection of resources on the Scottsboro Boys affair, complete with an overview, court records, maps of the crime scene, photographs, and links.

Bibliography

Adams, Phoebe. "*To Kill a Mockingbird*, by Harper Lee." *Atlantic Monthly*, August 1960. http://www. the atlantic. com/unbound/classrev/mocking.htm (accessed February 4, 2009).

Alabama Department of Archives and History. "The Great Depression, The New Deal, and Alabama's Political Leadership." *Alabama Moments in American History*. ADAH and The Friends of the Archives, 2001. http://www. alabamamoments.alabama.gov/sec48det.html (accessed February 4, 2009).

Bellafante, Ginia. "Harper Lee, Gregarious for a Day." *New York Times*, January 30, 2006. http://www. nytimes.com/2006/01/30/books/30lee.html?_r=2&oref=sl ogin&oref=slogin (accessed February 4, 2009).

Blackall, Jean Frantz. "Valorizing the Commonplace: Harper Lee's Response to Jane Austen." In Petry, *On Harper Lee*, 19–34.

Burstein, Patricia. "Tiny Yes, But a Terror?" *People*, May 10, 1976. http://www.people.com/people/archive/ article/0,,20066445,00.html (accessed February 4, 2009).

Chalfin, Richard. "The Day Harper Lee Came to See Me." *New York Observer*, December 3, 2000. http://www. observer.com/node/43707 (accessed February 4, 2009).

Childress, Mark. "Looking for Harper Lee." *Southern Living*, May 1997, 148–150.

Chura, Patrick. "Prolepsis and Anachronism: Emmett Till and the Historicity of *To Kill a Mockingbird*." *Southern Literary Journal* 32.2 (Spring 2000): 1–26.

Clarke, Gerald. *Capote: A Biography*. New York: Simon and Schuster, 1988.

———. *Too Brief a Treat: The Letters of Truman Capote*. New York: Random House, 2004.

Davis, Deborah. *Party of the Century: The Fabulous Story of Truman Capote and His Black and White Ball*. Hoboken, NJ: John Wiley and Sons, 2007.

Freedman, Monroe H. "Atticus Finch—Right and Wrong." *Alabama Law Review* 45 (2003–2004): 473+. Reprinted in Mancini, *Racism in Harper Lee's "To Kill a Mockingbird"*, 67–76.

Garbarino, Steve. "Greetings from Monroeville." *Black Book*, July 30, 2007. http://www.blackbookmag.com/article/greetings-from-monroeville2/996 (accessed February 4, 2009).

Grobel, Lawrence. *Conversations with Capote*. New York: New American Library, 1985.

Inge, M. Thomas. *Truman Capote: Conversations*. Jackson: University Press of Mississippi, 1987.

Johnson, Claudia Durst. *"To Kill a Mockingbird": Threatening Boundaries*. New York: Twayne, 1994.

Jones, George Thomas. *Happenings in Old Monroeville*. 2 vols. Monroeville, AL: Bolton Newspapers, 1999, 2003.

Kemp, Kathy. "Mockingbird Won't Sing." *News and Observer*, November 12, 1997. http://www.jlc.net/~rwright/pages/leearticle.html (accessed February 4, 2009).

Linder, Douglas O. "'The Scottsboro Boys' Trials." *Famous American Trials*. 1999. http://www.law.umkc.edu/faculty/ projects/ftrials/scottsboro/scottsb.htm (accessed February 4, 2009).

"Literary Laurels from a Novice." *Life*, May 26, 1961, 78A–78B.

Lyell, Frank H. "One-Taxi Town: *To Kill a Mockingbird*." *New York Times Book Review*, July 10, 1960.

Mancini, Candace. *Racism in Harper Lee's "To Kill a Mockingbird."* Farmington Hills, MI: Greenhaven Press, 2008.

McDonald, W. U. Jr. "Harper Lee's College Writings." *American Notes & Queries* 6.9 (May 1968): 131–133.

Mills, Marja. "To Find a Mockingbird." *Chicago Tribune*, December 28, 2002. http://www.smh.com.au/articles/2002/12/27/1040511175523.html (accessed February 4, 2009).

Moates, Marianne M. *A Bridge of Childhood: Truman Capote's Southern Years*. New York: Henry Holt, 1989.

Monroeville: The Search for Harper Lee's Maycomb. Charleston, SC: Arcadia Publishing, 1999.

Nance, William L. *The Worlds of Truman Capote*. New York: Stein and Day, 1970.

Newquist, Roy, ed. "Harper Lee." Interview by Roy Newquist, 403–412. *Counterpoint*. Chicago: Rand McNally, 1964.

Petry, Alice Hall. *On Harper Lee*. Knoxville: University of Tennessee Press, 2007.

Plimpton, George. *Truman Capote: In Which Various Friends, Enemies, Acquaintances and Detractors Recall His Turbulent Career*. New York: Doubleday, 1997.

Rudisill, Marie, and James C. Simmons. *Truman Capote: The Story of His Bizarre and Exotic Boyhood by an Aunt Who Helped Raise Him*. New York: William Morrow and Company, 1983.

Saney, Isaac. "The Case Against *To Kill a Mockingbird*." *Race & Class* 45 (July 2003): 99–100. Reprinted in Mancini, *Racism in Harper Lee's "To Kill a Mockingbird,"* 46–54.

Shields, Charles J. *Mockingbird: A Portrait of Harper Lee*. New York: Henry Holt, 2006.

Steinem, Gloria. "'Go Right Ahead and Ask Me Anything.' And So She Did. An Interview with Truman Capote." *McCall's*, November 1967, 66–67+. Reprinted in Inge, *Truman Capote: Conversations*, 86–104.

Tramble, Nichelle D. "Full Circle: A Personal Reflection." In Petry, *On Harper Lee*, 35–40.